T0369400

ACORNS FROM GOD

God's words for Personal Growth and Encouragement

Patti King

authorHOUSE®

AuthorHouse™ LLC
1663 Liberty Drive
Bloomington, IN 47403
www.authorhouse.com
Phone: 1-800-839-8640

© 2010, 2014 Patti King. All rights reserved.

No part of this book may be reproduced, stored in a retrieval system, or transmitted by any means without the written permission of the author.

Published by AuthorHouse   09/18/2014

ISBN: 978-1-4490-1186-4 (sc)
ISBN: 978-1-4490-1187-1 (hc)
ISBN: 978-1-4490-1188-8 (e)

Any people depicted in stock imagery provided by Thinkstock are models, and such images are being used for illustrative purposes only. Certain stock imagery © Thinkstock.

This book is printed on acid-free paper.

Because of the dynamic nature of the Internet, any web addresses or links contained in this book may have changed since publication and may no longer be valid. The views expressed in this work are solely those of the author and do not necessarily reflect the views of the publisher, and the publisher hereby disclaims any responsibility for them.

Excerpts from the New American Bible with Revised New Testament and Psalms *Copyright© 1991, 1986, 1970 by the Confraternity of Christian Doctrine, Washington, D.C. Used with permission. All Rights Reserved. No part of the* New American Bible *may be reproduced in any form without permission in writing from the copyright owner.*

For all those
who have "enfleshed"
the

Word of God
in my life,
this work is for
You!

ACKNOWLEDGEMENTS

So many years ago, a seed was sown into the fertile ground of my heart, and through the years this seed has grown into, **<u>Acorns from God</u>**. I have not done this by myself. Rather, many people have had a part in the creation of this precious book. These people have graced my life and inspired this work!

First, my husband, **Michael and beloved family** ...
And especially my daughter, **Julie**, who helped edit the pages.
Thank you for always supporting me with your *Love.*

To my **Mom** who has always encouraged me
to *Believe* in myself!

For my trinity of friends ...
Brenda-Lea, *Inspiration,*
the catalyst who first set me on this path
and went the distance to find the cover picture.

Deborah, a *Blessing* in my life,
who spent hours, weeks and so much more helping to edit the writing.
You brought a harvest of acorns with your wisdom and honesty.

Angela, my *Encourager,*
who has for years encouraged my creative inner self.
A true angel you have been to me.

For **all** those who have *prayed* for and encouraged me,
You are the wind beneath my wings.

For **those** whose pictures grace this book,
you bring *Life* to these words.

In *Thanksgiving* to **God,** who is the One who
planted the "acorn" and guided me along the way.

Each of you have brought your special touch that has made
a *Sacred* difference not only in this book, but my life!
Thank you!

You are Loved!

CONTENTS

INTRODUCTION

In the beginning was the Word,
and the Word was with God,
and the Word was God.
Jn. 1:1

In Scripture we have come to identify the "WORD of GOD" as JESUS! We *hear* the "WORD of GOD" every time the Scriptures are shared. We *feel* the "WORD of GOD" within the community through the loving touch of others. We *taste* the "WORD of GOD" in the Eucharist, through the transformation of the bread and the wine. As we have heard so many time, "We become what we eat." We *see* this "WORD of GOD" alive in all creation, in individuals who radiate Jesus, and in ourselves if we look very closely.

I would like to share with you a scripture passage that has always fascinated me:

One does not live by bread alone,
but by every word that comes forth
from the mouth of God.
Matt. 4:4

The phrase "every word" says a lot to me, ... not "THE Word" or "THIS Word," but "EVERY Word" that comes from the mouth of God. Little by little I began to see the power that each word had to change my life. My first word ever given to me was back in the '70s during a prayer meditation. Each of us was told to close our eyes and image a store, any store; and to go in and seek out that which we needed. I chose a favorite Christian store of mine known as "VIVA" bookstore. I went up and down the aisles of my imagination looking at objects, and searching for what "I WANTED." God had other plans. All of a sudden the word FAITH, in bold wooden letters, came out to me. It was as if they had a life of their own saying, "pick me!" But I said, "No,

I don't want FAITH." A little farther down, a symbol of faith pushed itself out in front … an ANCHOR of faith. And I again said no. As I tried to turn a corner in another aisle, the word FAITH was as huge as a person. I could not get around it and FAITH would not be put away. It was then that I truly understood. It wasn't about what I wanted, but what "I NEEDED." And God knew best! I sat and literally cried like a wayward child. I asked God to help me see how I needed FAITH and to help me take that word and make it my own.

Each WORD from God is like an acorn fallen from the oak tree. An acorn doesn't look like much, little and hard crusted! However, within this acorn lies all the DNA to become a mighty tree. I never paid much attention to acorns. Squirrels and deer loved to eat the acorns, and the children love to throw them! But my wise husband planted some acorns for our future trees around our new home (28 years ago.) At the time I laughed and said, "We will never have shade. It will take forever." He just smilingly ignored me, like God would do, and watered those acorns. Throughout the seasons of the years, the dry and wet times, those acorns did grow to be beautiful trees. Today they shelter the birds, and provide shade from the sun. Although our daughters did not enjoy these trees, 28 years later their children are swinging from the branches! When I look upon these trees I am reminded that my husband understood the value of time and patience. These precious oaks are a visual reminder to trust in God's ways!

This resource has helped me to "crawl into the acorn" and really dwell with the word. Inside, I found a sacred place where my spirit would find quiet rest and adventure. When all else around me was confused and agitated, … here I would find peace … and like the acorn … I grew!

Our loving Creator tells us:
> *May my instruction soak in like the rain,*
> *and my discourse permeate like the dew,*
> *Like a downpour upon the grass,*
> *like a shower upon the crops.*
> *Deut. 32:2*

Let each word soak into our hearts, our minds, and into the very marrow of our bones! And God promises:

For just as from the heavens
the rain and snow come down
And do not return there
till they have watered the earth,
making it fertile and fruitful,
Giving seed to him who sows
and bread to him who eats,
So shall my word be
that goes forth from my mouth;
It shall not return to me void,
but shall do my will,
achieving the end for which I sent it.
Is. 55:10-11

Each and every word is like an acorn, waiting to be planted deep in our hearts. There they will be watered and nurtured by God. If only we will be patient and open, and as a precious spiritual guide always said, "and let God have God's way."

In this creative endeavor, I have compiled 40 words which I feel have the power to challenge, affirm, and strengthen every seeker who is willing to travel this journey. These words are not to be read from beginning to end like any other book. Rather, prayerfully ask God for which WORD you NEED. And when guided to that word, let it soak into your heart. Let it breathe within you. Live with it for awhile. I spent a whole season of Lent with the word GLORY, or a summer with the word TRUST. Many people who first received their word, wanted to push it away; however, after living with it for a long while, embraced it and saw themselves in a new light!

May these words bring you ever closer to the ONE who created you and desires for you more than you could ever imagine!

Let the word of Christ dwell in you richly, as in all wisdom.
Col. 3:16

You are Loved!

Journeying with the Words

As you begin, you might decide to start a **journal** so that you collect your thoughts and experiences in one place. Journals are so important to writing down your thoughts and your feelings. God reveals the most unexpected truths within your writing. It is also a good place to use colored pencils or markers to "image your word." Allow your creative side to come forth.

Will you journey by **yourself or with a group**? Either way is good. A group can affirm each other throughout the decided time frame. The season of Lent or Advent, a season of summer, or perhaps simply 6 weeks. Whichever way you go, choose only one word for a period of time. You will be surprised how much one word can teach you! Do not hurry the process.

Creatively decide how you will let a word choose you! You could write each word on a piece of paper, a rock, or whatever you choose. We have used hearts, feathers, bookmarks and leaves. There are endless possibilities, so be creative. Turn the written objects over so that the word cannot be seen. Then open yourself in prayer, asking God to give you what you need. Trust the process. Choose one object, and turn it over to reveal your word. I really like using something tangible, something that will remind you of your word.

Prayer is where we begin and where we return if the Spirit is to guide us on this journey. Each of us should create a **special prayer place** where we can bring ourselves out of the busyness of life and be still. Like a farmer who tills the soil to prepare the soil to receive the seeds, so too do we need God to prepare our hearts to receive God's word for us. Simply show up with the right intention and God will do the rest. **Choose a time** when you will quiet yourself to listen to God and be renewed in the word. Remember, it takes a season for the seed to germinate, and mature. Nature is not to be hurried and neither is the "Word" in our life.

Humbly welcome the word.
James 1:21

Stay with a word at least a day; but do not be afraid to linger into a week or month. There is no time table. Simply dwell with the word. I find choosing one scripture passage at a time (day, week,) gives me a different insight into the word and me.

If you care to write:
Do not answer all the questions at one sitting ... take your time.
This process is about going deep. So take
one question and work with it
for a while. You do not have to know the
answers to find truth for yourself. Just
write, brainstorm, whatever come to your mind.
Walk away and later come back to it.
Let the Spirit bring more questions to your heart.

What does this word mean to me?
How does this word challenge me?
How does receiving this word at this time ... affirm me?
               "   ... challenge me to grow
                                              with this word?
               "   ... strengthen me at this
                                              time?
Who in my life has the qualities of this word?
What does this word say about God?
What does this word reveal about me?
Write a poem or song about this word.

If you care to draw the word:
Looking at this word, what color comes to mind?
What does this word look like?
What symbols describe this word?

Where is God in the picture?
What does the drawing reveal about me?

Live this word:
What difference does it make for me to live this word?
Do a creative action that comes from this word.
Create a collage about this word.
Make a dance.
Share the message of this word with someone who needs it.

Do not be afraid to **use all forms of a word**. For instance: **Call, called, calling.** Each form can take us into a deeper understanding of the word within ourselves! Looking at a word from many angles can lead us from yesterday, to today, and then to tomorrow. Like the many ways to view a beautiful cut diamond … explore! You never know what may be revealed to you.

**As you come to see this word in yourself and can claim it …
CELEBRATE the Word and give thanks!**

****

Receiving the Word

(This is just an example of a prayer service. Be creative.)

Have the **Words** placed around the altar area, altar cloth, candle, bible. Each word may be placed on the back of a piece of paper, an object, or whatever you creatively choose.

Opening Song: "Be Still" by David Kauffman from the CD titled, Be Still.

Opening Prayer: Let us place ourselves in the presence of our God.

> Abba, we come open and ready to sit in your presence,
> that you may plant Your Word deep within us.
> We trust that You know us better than we know ourselves.
> You will give us what we need and we are grateful. Amen.

Scripture: Isaiah 55:10-11

> For just as from the heavens
> the rain and snow come down
> And do not return there
> till they have watered the earth ...
> So shall my word be
> that goes forth from my mouth;
> It shall not return to me void,
> but shall do my will,
> achieving the end for which I sent it.

Explanation: The Hebrew people saw the Word of God as alive and active, transforming the one who hears. The Word was not written for a long time but rather memorized and passed on from generation to generation. Just as Isaiah says, the word will not return to God until it has achieved the end for which it was given.

We have prayed over these words that at the right time, each word will be chosen by the right person. May it be for you like bread that nourishes the body, until that word is ...You!

In the quiet stillness ... we begin.

Let us pray:

Lord, we come to you.
Although we have our fears & anxieties,
we desire so strongly to serve you and
learn from you ... that we come.
We leave our comfortable hiding places
and come out into Your light.
We ask you to bless these words
and open our hearts to receive
that which you will plant there,
... our word!
Accept our littleness
and make of us what you will.
We pray in the name of Jesus our Lord.
Amen.

With quiet background music (no words).

One person to call each by name. One at a time. (Have a roster in place.)
Receiver of the word selects one of the words from the altar and goes to ...
Someone to affirm the person with their chosen word & pray with them.
Someone writes down the person's name & their word.
   (You wouldn't believe how often people forget their own word.)

After all have received their word.

Claim your word … using your word … give thanks to God in a single sentence.

> (or a simple sharing, for example: "God has given me love, and I really need to feel loved at this time.")

Closing Song: "I Think of You with Love" by David Kauffman, from the CD titled Surrender

ACORNS FROM GOD

"The Words"

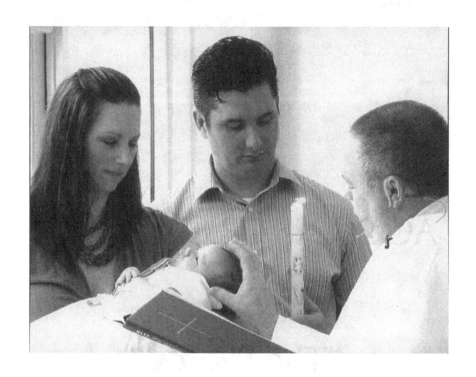

ANOINTED

In the holy anointing of Baptism,
each of us is claimed by God,
and made sacred.
How is it that we forget that so easily?

Patti King

ANOINTED

"Anoint," as I have come to know it means: to bless, to set aside as sacred, as belonging to God. There is the story in scripture about Jacob and his encounter with God. One night he lays his head down to sleep and has a dream about God that so moves him, that when he wakes, he says,

Truly, the Lord is in this spot, although I did not know it!
Genesis 28:16

He sets up a memorial stone and pours oil over it, to bless it and mark it as sacred; and he calls it Bethel. (Bethel is Hebrew for ... House of God.)

That story can help us to understand what happens when we have been anointed in Baptism and Confirmation. The sacred oil marks us as holy for always. If only we truly understood that God desires us and chooses to dwell with us. God does not come to us because we are so good. Rather, we are good because God is within us!

Once in a prayer service a special woman received the word Anointed. She was disturbed to her very soul because she felt that she was not worthy. After 13 weeks of walking with this word, she saw herself very differently ... a little more like God sees her. Oh the power of the word. How much more the power of the action!

Image if you will, the holy oils used for sacramental anointing. The precious oils are held in clear glass for all to see. God's radiant light comes shining through the window passing through the oils. The resulting golden amber glow casts its color upon you. Be bathed in the golden glow of God's love. Remember, for those anointed in Baptism, God has set you aside as belonging to God, sacred and precious!

Let the word lead you to see yourself as God
sees you … the anointed of God!

Reflection questions:

In the Old Testament priests, prophets and kings were anointed.

So what does that say about you … a baptized, confirmed Christian?

How can you better live out this "anointing" in your everyday life?

ANOINTED

Gen. 28:16, 18-19 When Jacob awoke from his sleep, he exclaimed, "Truly, the Lord is in this spot, although I did not know it." Early the next morning Jacob took the stone that he had put under his head, set it up as a memorial stone, and poured oil on top of it. He called that site Bethel.

Lev. 8:10, 12 Taking the anointing oil, Moses anointed and consecrated the Dwelling, with all that was in it. He also poured some of the anointing oil on Aaron's head, thus consecrating him.

1 Sam. 2:35 I will choose a faithful priest who shall do what I have in heart and mind. I will establish a lasting house for him which shall function in the presence of my anointed forever.

1 Sam. 15:17-18a Samuel then said: "Though little in your own esteem, are you not leader of the tribes of Israel? The Lord anointed you king of Israel and sent you on a mission."

1 Sam. 16:12-13 The LORD said, "There—anoint him, for this is he!" Then Samuel, with the horn of oil in hand, anointed him in the midst of his brothers; and from that day on, the spirit of the Lord rushed upon David.

2 Chr. 6:42 LORD God, reject not the plea of your anointed, / remember the devotion of David your servant.

Ps. 20:7 Now I know victory is given / to the anointed of the LORD. / God will answer him from the holy heavens / with a strong arm that brings victory.

Ps. 23:5-6   You set a table before me / as my enemies watch; / You anoint my head with oil; /my cup overflows. / Only goodness and love will pursue me /all the days of my life./ I will dwell in the house of the Lord / for years to come.

Ps. 28:8-9   LORD, you are the strength of your people, / the saving refuge of your anointed king. / Save your people, bless your inheritance; / feed and sustain them forever!

Ps. 45:8   You love justice and hate wrongdoing; / therefore God, your God, has anointed you / with the oil of gladness.

Ps. 84:10   O God, look kindly on our shield; / look upon the face of your anointed.

Ps. 89:21   I have chosen David, my servant; / with my holy oil I have anointed him.

Ps. 92:11   You have given me the strength of a wild bull; / you have poured rich oil upon me.

Ps. 132:17   I will set a lamp for my anointed.

Is. 45:1   Thus says the LORD to his anointed, Cyrus, / whose right hand I grasp, / Subduing nations before him, / and making kings run to his service, / Opening doors before him / and leaving the gates unbarred.

Is. 61:1   The spirit of the Lord GOD is upon me, / because the LORD has anointed me. / He has sent me to bring glad tidings to the lowly, / to heal the brokenhearted, / To proclaim liberty to the captives / and release to prisoners.

Hab. 3:13   You come forth to save your people, / to save your anointed one.

Matt. 6:17-18   When you fast, anoint your head and wash your face, so that you may not appear to be fasting, except to your Father who is hidden. And your Father who sees what is hidden will repay you.

Mk. 6:13   They drove out many demons, and they anointed with oil many who were sick and cured them.

Lk. 4:18-19   The Spirit of the Lord is upon me, / because he has anointed me / to bring glad tidings to the poor. / He has sent me to proclaim liberty to captives / and recovery of sight to the blind, / to let the oppressed go free, / and to proclaim a year acceptable to the Lord.

Lk. 7:46-47   You did not anoint my head with oil, but she anointed my feet with ointment. So I tell you, her many sins have been forgiven, hence, she has shown great love.

Jn. 9:11   "The man called Jesus made clay and anointed my eyes and told me, 'Go to Siloam and wash.' So I went there and washed and was able to see."

Jn. 11:2   Mary was the one who had anointed the Lord with perfumed oil and dried his feet with her hair; it was her brother Lazarus who was ill.

Jn. 12:3   Mary took a liter of costly perfumed oil made from genuine aromatic nard and anointed the feet of Jesus and dried them with her hair, the house was filled with the fragrance of the oil.

Acts 10:36-38   You know the word [that] he sent to the Israelites as he proclaimed peace through Jesus Christ, who is Lord of all, what happened all over Judea beginning in Galilee after the baptism that John preached, how God anointed Jesus of Nazareth with the holy Spirit and power.

2 Cor. 1:21-22   But the one who gives us security with you in Christ and who anointed us is God; he has also put his seal upon us and given the Spirit in our hearts as a first installment.

1Jn. 2:20   You have the anointing that comes from the holy one, and you all have knowledge.

1Jn. 2:27   As for you, the anointing that you received from him remains in you, so that you do not need anyone to teach you. But his anointing teaches you about everything and is true and not false; just as it taught you, remain in him.

BELIEVE

I believe that God is in me
as the sun is in the
color and fragrance of a flower,
the light in my darkness,
the voice in my silence.

Helen Keller

Believe

When asked, "Do you believe?", we probably would reply, "Sure." If asked again, "Do you really believe?", we might step back and realize that we too have our doubts. Almost everything I used to believe throughout the years has been tested and found wanting. From the realization that our childhood fantasies are not real, to the adult fantasies that life is fair and love is forever! We are a lot more like Doubting Thomas than we care to admit. I am encouraged by the scripture verse:

I do believe, help my unbelief.
Mk. 9:24

So what do I believe in?

I believe in God, the one who created me; in Jesus, who is the Way, the Truth and the Life; and in the Spirit who teaches me to dance my faith. I believe in love and its endless possibilities for healing the world. I believe that people are intrinsically good although they often seem the worse for the wear, because of their pains and hurts. I am an unfinished work of art by the Creator and I believe that God is still molding me. I may not fully understand, but God is helping me along the way. I discovered, when my belief is lacking, I can lean on the strength and wisdom of the faith community!

When will we know when we truly believe? The strength of our belief will be apparent when we stand firm and tall like a giant oak tree for all to see. When we truly give voice to what needs to be said; instead of remaining quiet. When people simply have to look at us because we are not just "talking the talk," but we are "walking the walk!"

May our lives resound an "AMEN" to the
question ..."Do you really believe?"

Reflection Questions:

What do you believe in? (Write you own personal creed. This activity may help you to see where you are strong in your belief, and where you are still growing in faith.)

What or who helps you in your unbelief?

BELIEVE

Ps. 27: 13 I believe I shall enjoy the LORD's goodness / in the land of the living.

Wis. 12:17 For you show your might when the perfection of your power is disbelieved; / and in those who know you, you rebuke temerity.

Wis. 16:26 That your sons whom you loved might learn, O LORD, / that it is not the various kinds of fruits that nourish man, / but it is your word that preserves those who believe you!

Is. 43:10 You are my witnesses, says the LORD, / my servants whom I have chosen / To know and believe in me.

Hab. 1:5 Look over the nations and see, / and be utterly amazed! / For a work is being done in your days / that you would not have believed, were it told.

Mt. 8:13 You may go; as you have believed, let it be done for you.

Mt. 9:28 "Do you believe that I can do this?" "Yes, Lord," they said to him.

Mt. 18:6 Whoever causes one of these little ones who believe in me to sin, it would be better for him to have a great millstone hung around his neck and to be drowned in the depths of the sea.

Mk. 1:15 This is the time of fulfillment. The kingdom of God is at hand. Repent, and believe in the gospel.

Mk. 9:24 I do believe, help my unbelief!

Mk. 11:23	Amen, I say to you, whoever says to this mountain, "Be lifted up and thrown into the sea" and does not doubt in his heart but believes that what he says will happen, it shall be done for him.
Mk. 11:24	Therefore I tell you, all that you ask for in prayer, believe that you will receive it and it shall be yours.
Lk. 1:45	Blessed are you who believed that what was spoken to you by the Lord would be fulfilled.
Jn. 1:7	He came for testimony, to testify to the light, so that all might believe through him.
Jn. 1:12	But to those who did accept him he gave power to become children of God, to those who believe in his name.
Jn. 3:16	For God so loved the world that he gave his only Son, so that everyone who believes in him might not perish but might have eternal life.
Jn. 4:21	Believe me, woman, the hour is coming when you will worship the Father neither on this mountain nor in Jerusalem.
Jn. 5:24	Amen, amen, I say to you, whoever hears my word and believes in the one who sent me has eternal life and will not come to condemnation, but has passed from death to life
Jn. 5:44	How can you believe, when you accept praise from one another and do not seek the praise that comes from the only God?
Jn. 6:29	Jesus answered and said to them, "This is the work of God, that you believe in the one he sent."

Jn. 6:35	Jesus said to them; "I am the bread of life; whoever comes to me will never hunger and whoever believes in me will never thirst."
Jn. 6:40	For this is the will of my Father, that everyone who sees the Son and believes in him may have eternal life, and I shall raise him [on] the last day.
Jn. 6:68-69	Master, to whom shall we go? You have the words of eternal life. We have come to believe and are convinced that you are the Holy One of God.
Jn. 7:38	Whoever believes in me, as scripture says: / "Rivers of living water will flow from within him."
Jn. 8:31	Jesus said to those Jews who believed in him, "If you remain in my word, you will know the truth, and the truth will set you free."
Jn. 9:38	I do believe, Lord!
Jn. 10:38	If I perform them, even if you do not believe me, believe the works, so that you may realize [and understand] that the Father is in me and I am in the Father.
Jn. 11:25-26	I am the resurrection and the life; whoever believes in me, even if he dies, will live, and everyone who lives and believes in me will never die.
Jn.11:27	"Yes, Lord. I have come to believe that you are the Messiah, the Son of God, the one who is coming into the world."
Jn. 11:40	Did I not tell you that if you believe you will see the glory of God?

Jn. 12:36   While you have the light, believe in the light, so that you may become children of the light.

Jn. 12:46   I came into the world as light, so that everyone who believes in me might not remain in darkness.

Jn. 14:11   Believe me that I am in the Father and the Father is in me, or else, believe because of the works themselves.

Jn. 14:12   Amen, amen, I say to you, whoever believes in me will do the works that I do, and will do greater ones than these, because I am going to the Father.

Jn. 16:27   For the Father himself loves you, because you have loved me and have come to believe that I came from God.

Jn. 17:20   I pray not only for them, but also for those who will believe in me through their word.

Jn. 17:21   … so that they may all be one, as you, Father, are in me and I in you, that they also may be in us, that the world may believe that you sent me.

Jn. 20:29   Have you come to believe because you have seen me? Blessed are those who have not seen and have believed.

Acts 2:44   All who believed were together and had all things in common.

Acts 4:32   The community of believers was of one heart and mind, and no one claimed that any of his possessions was his own, but they had everything in common.

Acts 10:43   To him all the prophets bear witness, that everyone who believes in him will receive forgiveness of sins through his name.

Acts 15:11	We believe that we are saved through the grace of the Lord Jesus.
Acts 16:31	"Believe in the Lord Jesus and you and your household will be saved."
Rom. 6:8	If, then, we have died with Christ, we believe that we shall also live with him.
Rom. 10:9	If you confess with your mouth that Jesus is Lord and believe in your heart that God raised him from the dead, you will be saved.
Rom. 10:10	For one believes with the heart and so is justified, and one confesses with the mouth and so is saved.
Rom. 10:11	No one who believes in him will be put to shame.
Rom. 15:13	May the God of hope fill you with all joy and peace in believing, so that you may abound in hope by the power of the holy Spirit.
1Cor. 13:7	[Love] bears all things, believes all things, hopes all things, endures all things.
Eph. 1:13	In him you also, who have heard the word of truth, the gospel of your salvation, and have believed in him, were sealed with the promised holy Spirit.
Phil. 1:29	For to you has been granted, for the sake of Christ, not only to believe in him but also to suffer for him.
1 Th. 2:13	And for this reason we too give thanks to God unceasingly, that, in receiving the word of God from hearing us, you received not a human word but, as it truly is, the word of God, which is now at work in you who believe.

1 Tim. 4:10   For this we toil and struggle, because we have set our hope on the living God, who is the savior of all, especially of those who believe.

1 Tim. 4:12   Let no one have contempt for your youth, but set an example for those who believe, in speech, conduct, love, faith, and purity.

2 Tim. 1:12   On this account I am suffering these things; but I am not ashamed, for I know him in whom I have believed and am confident that he is able to guard what has been entrusted to me until that day.

Heb. 11:6   But without faith it is impossible to please him, for anyone who approaches God must believe that he exists and that he rewards those who seek him.

Ja.2:23   Thus the scripture was fulfilled that says: "Abraham believed God, and it was credited to him as righteousness."

1 Pet. 1:8   Although you have not seen him you love him; even though you do not see him now, yet believe in him, you rejoice with an indescribable and glorious joy.

1Jn. 3:23   And his commandment is this: we should believe in the name of his Son, Jesus Christ, and love one another just as he commanded us.

1Jn. 4:16   We have come to know and to believe in the love God has for us.

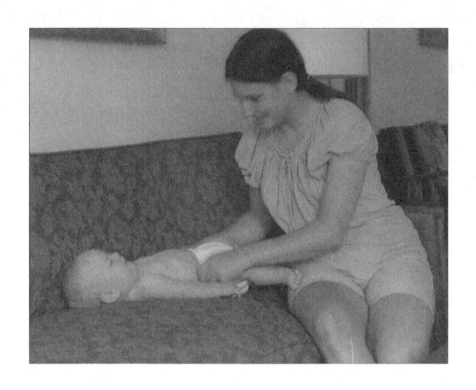

BELOVED

And you, O Father,
bend lovingly over your poor little creature,
"cover her with your shadow,"
seeing in her only the
"beloved in whom you are well pleased."

Blessed Elizabeth of the Trinity

BELOVED

Beloved is a word that for many may seem more like a "fairy tale." Traveling through life, we often can become cynical and distrusting of truly being loved. What would it mean to be the beloved … the one being loved; the person that was set aside and given that individual focus of love from another? Isn't that what we all hope for? How many people enter marriage not really believing that it will last?

What if the other person were God, loving us? We need to examine our image of God. If I image God as a judge, especially one that is keeping track of all my mistakes, I might find it hard to see God as truly loving me. However, if I can see God as a loving Shepherd, who leaves the ninety-nine others to come find me, then I might understand how God loves me with an abandon … as I am!

Can I also look upon my gracious and faithful God and return that look of love? Can I accept God as God is, and not demand that God be what I want God to be, or do what I want God to do? Can I see God as the Beloved of my heart?

The day I first realized that God saw me as the beloved of God's heart …WOW! What a difference that made in my life! Everything seemed clearer and easier. Loving God is a joy! Learning to see myself as God sees me, well that was the greater challenge … that I am loveable.

Choose one of those special evenings when the sunset seems to stop time, and you just want drink it all in. Quiet yourself so that only your breathing remains and let the soft glow of the sunset warm you. Open your heart to the presence of the One who loves you, the One who created you to be, the Beloved; and with a single-mindedness between the two of you … just be!

Patti King

Reflection Questions:

What is your image of God?

What difference would it make in your life if you truly felt "beloved"?

Knowing God does see you this way, what needs to change in you to believe it?

BELOVED

Deut. 33:12   Benjamin is the beloved of the LORD, / who shelters him all the day, / while he abides securely at his breast.

Ps. 127:2   It is vain for you to rise early /and put off your rest at night. / To eat bread earned by hard toil - / all this God gives to his beloved in sleep.

So. 2:10   My lover speaks; he says to me, / "Arise, my beloved, my beautiful one, / and come!"

So. 4:1   Ah, you are beautiful, my beloved, / ah, you are beautiful!

So. 4:7   You are all-beautiful, my beloved, / and there is no blemish in you.

Dan. 9:23   When you began your petition, an answer was given which I have come to announce, because you are beloved.

Dan. 10:11   "Daniel, beloved," he said to me, "understand the words which I am speaking to you; stand up, for my mission now is to you."

Dan. 10:19   Fear not, beloved, you are safe; take courage and be strong!

Matt. 17:5   While he was still speaking, behold, a bright cloud cast a shadow over them, then from the cloud came a voice that said, "This is my beloved Son, with whom I am well pleased; listen to him."

Mk. 1:11   And a voice came from the heavens, "You are my beloved Son, with you I am well pleased."

Rom. 1:7	… to all the beloved of God in Rome, called to be holy. Grace to you and peace from God our Father and the Lord Jesus Christ.
Rom. 9:25	As indeed he says in Hosea: / "Those who were not my people, I will call 'my people,'/ and her who was not beloved, I will call 'beloved.' … "
1Cor. 15:58	Therefore, my beloved brothers, be firm, steadfast, always fully devoted to the work of the Lord, knowing that in the Lord your labor is not in vain.
2 Cor. 7:1	Since we have these promises, beloved, let us cleanse ourselves from every defilement of flesh and spirit, making holiness perfect in the fear of God.
Eph. 1:5-6	… he destined us for adoption to himself through Jesus Christ, in accord with the favor of his will, for the praise of the glory of his grace that he granted us in the beloved.
Eph. 5:1-2	So be imitators of God, as beloved children, and live in love, as Christ loved us.
Phil. 4:1	Therefore, my brothers and sisters, whom I love and long for, my joy and crown, in this way stand firm in the Lord, beloved.
Col. 3:12-13	Put on then, as God's chosen ones, holy and beloved, heartfelt compassion, kindness, humility, gentleness and patience, bearing with one another and forgiving one another.
Ja.1:16	Do not be deceived, my beloved brothers: all good giving and every perfect gift is from above.
1Pe. 2:11	Beloved, I urge you as aliens and sojourners to keep away from worldly desires that wage war against the soul.

1Pe. 4:12-13	Beloved, do not be surprised that a trial by fire is occurring among you, as if something strange were happening to you. But rejoice to the extent that you share in the sufferings of Christ, so that when his glory is revealed you may also rejoice exultantly.
2 Pe. 3:14	Therefore beloved, since you await these things, be eager to be found without spot or blemish before him, at peace.
1 Jo. 3:2	Beloved, we are God's children now; what we shall be has not yet been revealed. We do know that when it is revealed we shall be like him, for we shall see him as he is.
1 Jo. 3:21	Beloved, if [our] hearts do not condemn us, we have confidence in God.
1 Jo. 4:7	Beloved, let us love one another, because love is of God.
1 Jo. 4:11-12	Beloved, if God so loved us, we also must love one another. No one has ever seen God. Yet, if we love one another, God remains in us, and his love is brought to perfection in us.
3 Jo. 2	Beloved, I hope you are prospering in every respect and are in good health, just as your soul is prospering.
3 Jo. 5	Beloved, you are faithful in all you do.
Jude 20-21	But you, beloved, build yourselves up in your most holy faith; pray in the holy spirit. Keep yourselves in the love of God and wait for the mercy of our Lord Jesus Christ that leads to eternal life.

BLESSED

A birthed bundle
surprised into life,
light filling the center
of a new spirit;
the blessing of eternity
passed on ...

Joyce Rupp

BLESSED

How often in our lives have we said, "I was really lucky!" Never realizing that the Giver of all gifts, desires to bless us with so much; even the simplest things that we hadn't even thought to ask for. We probably do not feel that we "deserve" to be blessed. Yet the more I come to know God, the more I realize that God loves with unconditional love. God does not give to us because we deserve it; but because God loves us so much, he desires to lavish us with all that is good!

We look around and say, "Well, it looks like God loves them more, look at how much they have!" Judging by worldly standards of wants and possessions we miss seeing our true blessings. God knows what will make us truly happy. If we but have the courage to look with "kingdom eyes" (to see as God sees), we would be amazed at how blessed we truly are everyday!

So how am I blessed? I am truly blessed with life, love, times of solitude, kingdom eyes to see, mercy, joy, a loving family and faithful friends. Not only am I blessed in the positive things of my life, but also the dark times, the difficult days, illness and pain. How you might ask? Ask God, "Lord, where is the blessing in this difficult time?" Usually the answer is: this is where you are strengthened, empowered, and encouraged. You would also discover that Jesus was with you all along!

The question really comes ... how do I respond to this generosity? Hopefully, we give thanks! We are also called to be a blessing to others, to be the reflection of a gracious and loving Creator. Now, that is an everyday journey ... learning to be a "blessing!"

Reflection Questions:

How are you blessed? Perhaps make a collage of all your blessings!

What ways might God be calling you to "be a blessing"?

BLESSED

Gen. 12:2 I will make your name great, / so that you will be a blessing.

Deut. 28:2-4a, 6 When you hearken to the voice of the LORD, your God, all these blessings will come upon you and overwhelm you:
"May you be blessed in the city,
    and blessed in the country!"
"Blessed be the fruit of your womb, … ."
"May you be blessed in your coming in,
    and blessed in your going out!"

Tobit 3:11 Blessed are you, O Lord, merciful God! / Forever blessed and honored is your holy name; /may all your works forever bless you!

Tobit 4:19 At all times bless the Lord God, and ask him to make all your paths straight and to grant success to all your endeavors and plans.

Tobit 8:15 Blessed are you, O God, with every holy and pure blessing! / Let all your chosen ones praise you; / let them praise you forever!

Tobit 8:16 Blessed are you, who have made me glad; / what I feared did not happen. / Rather you have dealt with us / according to your great mercy.

Tobit 11:17 "Welcome my daughter! Blessed be your God for bringing you to us, daughter! … Blessed are you, daughter! Welcome to your home with blessing and joy. Come in, daughter!"

Ps. 5:13	For you, LORD, bless the just; / you surround them with favor like a shield.
Ps. 16:7	I bless the LORD who counsels me; / even at night my heart exhorts me.
Ps. 18:47	The LORD lives! Blessed be my rock! / Exalted be God, my savior!
Ps. 21:3-4	You granted him his heart's desire; / you did not refuse the prayer of his lips. / For you welcomed him with goodly blessings; / you placed on his head a crown of pure gold.
Ps. 21:7	You make him the pattern of blessings forever, / you gladden him with the joy of your presence.
Ps. 24:4-5	The clean of hand and pure of heart; / ... They will receive blessings from the LORD / and justice from their saving God.
Ps. 28:6-7	Blessed be the LORD, / who has heard the sound of my pleading. / The LORD is my strength and my shield, / in whom my heart trusted and found help./ So my heart rejoices; / with my song I praise my God.
Ps. 28:8-9	LORD, you are the strength of your people, / the saving refuge of your anointed king. / Save your people, bless your inheritance; / feed and sustain them forever!
Ps. 29:11	May the LORD give might to his people; / may the LORD bless his people with peace.
Ps. 31:22	Blessed be the LORD, / who has shown me wondrous love!
Ps. 34:2	I will bless the LORD at all times; / praise shall be always in my mouth.

Ps. 63:5   I will bless you as long as I live; / I will lift up my hands, calling on your name.

Ps. 66:20   Blessed be God, who did not refuse me / the kindness I sought in prayer.

Ps. 67:2   May God be gracious to us and bless us; / may God's face shine upon us.

Ps. 68:36   Awesome is God in his holy place, / the God of Israel, / who gives power and strength to his people. / Blessed be God!

Ps. 103:1-2   Bless the LORD, my soul; / all my being, bless his holy name! / Bless the LORD, my soul; / do not forget all the gifts of God.

Ps. 104:1   Bless the LORD, my soul! / LORD, my God, you are great indeed!

Ps. 118:26   Blessed is he / who comes in the name of the LORD.

Ps. 133:1, 3   How good it is, how pleasant, / where the people dwell as one! / There the LORD has lavished blessings, / life for evermore.

Ps. 144:1   Blessed be the LORD, my Rock.

Ps. 144:15   Happy the people so blessed; / happy the people whose God is the LORD.

So. 6:12   Before I knew it, my heart had made me / the blessed one of my kinswomen.

Wis. 3:5   Chastised a little, they shall be greatly blessed, / because God tried them / and found them worthy of himself.

Sir. 1:11   He who fears the LORD will have a happy end; / even on the day of his death he will be blessed.

Sir. 45:26   And now bless the LORD / who has crowned you with glory! / May he grant you wisdom of heart.

Jer. 31:12   Shouting, they shall mount the heights of Zion, / they shall come streaming to the Lord's blessings./ ... They themselves shall be like watered gardens, / never again shall they languish.

Jer. 31:14   I will lavish choice portions upon the priests, / and my people shall be filled with my blessings, / says the Lord.

Da. 12:12   Blessed is the man who has patience and perseveres.

Mal. 3:10   Bring the whole tithe / into the storehouse, / That there may be food in my house, / and try me in this, says the Lord of hosts; / Shall I not open for you the floodgates of heaven, / to pour down blessing upon you without measure?

Matt. 5:3   Blessed are the poor in spirit, / for theirs is the kingdom of heaven.

Matt. 5:4   Blessed are they who mourn, / for they will be comforted.

Matt. 5:5   Blessed are the meek, / for they will inherit the land.

Matt. 5:6   Blessed are they that hunger and thirst for righteousness, / for they will be satisfied

Matt. 5:7   Blessed are the merciful, / for they will be shown mercy.

Matt. 5:8   Blessed are the clean of heart, / for they will see God.

Matt. 5:9   Blessed are the peacemakers, / for they will be called children of God.

Matt. 5:10   Blessed are they who are persecuted for the sake of righteousness, / for theirs is the kingdom of heaven.

Matt. 5:11-12   Blessed are you when they insult you and persecute you and utter every kind of evil against you [falsely] because of me. Rejoice and be glad, for your reward will be great in heaven.

Matt. 25:34   Come, you who are blessed by my Father. Inherit the kingdom prepared for you from the foundation of the world.

Lk. 1:42   Most blessed are you among women, and blessed is the fruit of your womb.

Lk. 1:45   Blessed are you who believed that was spoken to you by the Lord would be fulfilled.

Lk. 1:46-48   My soul proclaims the greatness of the Lord; / my spirit rejoices in God, my savior. / For he has looked upon his handmaid's lowliness; / behold, from now on all ages will call me blessed.

Lk. 6: 20   Blessed are you who are poor, / for the kingdom of God is yours.

Lk. 6: 21   Blessed are you who are now hungry, / for you will be satisfied. / Blessed are you who are now weeping, / for you will laugh.

Lk. 6:22-23   Blessed are you when people hate you, / and when they exclude and insult you, / and denounce your name as evil / on account of the Son of Man. / Rejoice and leap for joy on that day! Behold, your reward will be great in heaven.

Jo. 12: 13	Hosanna! / Blessed is he who comes in the name of the Lord.
Jo. 13:14, 17	If I therefore, the master and teacher, have washed your feet, you ought to wash one another's feet. If you understand this, blessed are you if you do it.
Acts 20:35	It is more blessed to give than to receive.
1Cor. 4:12	When ridiculed, we bless; when persecuted, we endure.
Eph. 1:3	Blessed be the God and Father of our Lord Jesus Christ, who has blessed us in Christ with every spiritual blessing in the heavens.
Ja. 1:12	Blessed is the one who perseveres in temptation, for when he has been proved he will receive the crown of life that he promised to those who love him.
Ja. 5:11	Indeed, we call blessed those who have persevered.
1Pe. 3:9	Do not return evil for evil, or insult for insult; but, on the contrary, a blessing, because to this you were called, that you might inherit a blessing.
1Pe. 3:14-15	But even if you should suffer because of righteousness, blessed are you. Do not be afraid or terrified with fear of them, but sanctify Christ as Lord in your hearts.
1Pe. 4:14	If you are insulted for the name of Christ, blessed are you, for the Spirit of glory and of God rests upon you.

CALLED

I was called
by Love to respond in love ...
by Light to be light ...
by Forgiveness to forgive ...
by Compassion to be compassionate...
by Mercy to be merciful ...
by Humility to be humble ...
by Joy to be a person of joy ...
by Truth to live in truth ...
by Sacred Presence to be a sacred presence ...
By the Heart of God
That my heart may hold God's people.
And I said YES!

Patti King

CALLED

Long ago I learned that you can ask for volunteers, but the need is filled greater when you "call someone by name." To be called by name speaks to a deeper part of our self that wants to be recognized and needed.

It is easy to see Abraham, Samuel, Jacob, Moses and all the disciples being "called" by God. They were holy people, "perfect for the mission" … or were they? Abraham was an old, old man. Samuel was a mere youth. Jacob stole his brother's inheritance. Moses killed a man. The disciples were fishermen and a tax collector … need I say more?

And how did God call them? Abraham had visions and three visitors on an ordinary day. Samuel heard God in his sleep, (the only time most of us are quiet enough to listen!) Jacob experienced God in his dreams and Moses heard a voice from the burning bush. While they were at work the disciples heard Jesus call to them to "*follow.*" Did any of them understand what God was asking of them? NO. Did they truly understand the promises? NO. Someplace deep within themselves there may have been this encouragement to simply "trust," they followed and said YES.

The first time God tugged at my heartstrings and I thought I heard a call, I responded immediately, "Me? Couldn't be!" Then came the excuses, and I had lots of them! It seems that God has to repeat the call at least three times before I get it. When God calls me, it's not like I get hit by lightening. He may send signals to me in different forms such as receiving a telephone call, running into someone in a grocery store, or listening to a special sermon that seems to be meant just for me. However, just because I receive a phone call does not mean that it is from God. Discernment in prayer is needed to see if this is where God is leading me, or is it simply others who want me in on their ventures? To be ready for God, we need to be careful not to get too busy with other things.

What about you? What ways has God called you in the past … in the scriptures, church community, family, marriage, sickness, death, in the dark of the night or in the bright light of day? Or did you play hide and seek with God so you didn't have to hear?

Oh, to simply be aware of God calling us out of ourselves, into God's wonderful love! Calling us to be greater than we are! Calling us into oneness with God!

Reflection Questions:
Have you experienced God calling you? When?
If not, what may be blocking your ability to hear?
Does being called by God make a difference in how you live your life? Explain.

CALLED

Gen. 17:5	No longer shall you be called Abram; your name shall be Abraham, for I am making you the father of a host of nations.
Gen. 35:10	"You whose name is Jacob / shall no longer be called Jacob, / but Israel shall be your name."
1 Sam. 3:10	The LORD came and revealed his presence, calling out as before, "Samuel, Samuel!" Samuel answered, "Speak, for your servant is listening!"
2 Sam. 22:7	In my distress I called upon the LORD / and cried out to my God; / From his temple he heard my voice, / and my cry reached his ears.
Ps. 4:2	Answer when I call, my saving God. / In my troubles, you cleared a way; / show me favor; hear my prayer.
Ps. 4: 4	Know that the LORD works wonders for the faithful; / the LORD hears when I call out.
Ps. 17:6	I call upon you; answer me, O God./ Turn your ear to me; hear my prayer.
Ps. 50:15	Then call on me in time of distress, / I will rescue you, and you shall honor me.
Ps. 63:5	I will bless you as long as I live; / I will lift up my hands, calling on your name.
Ps. 86:5	Lord, you are kind and forgiving, / most loving to all who call on you.

Ps. 91:15	All who call upon me I will answer; / I will be with them in distress; / I will deliver them and give them honor.
Ps. 116:1-2	I love the LORD, who listened / to my voice in supplication, / Who turned an ear to me / on the day I called.
Ps. 118:5	In danger I called on the LORD; / the LORD answered me and set me free.
Ps. 130:1-2	Out of the depths I call to you, LORD; / Lord, hear my cry!
Ps. 141:1	LORD, I call to you; / come quickly to help me; / listen to my plea when I call.
Ps. 145:18	You, LORD, are near to all who call upon you, / to all who call upon you in truth.
Is. 41:9-10	You whom I have taken from the ends of the earth / and summoned from its far-off places, / You whom I have called my servant, / whom I have chosen and will not cast off-- / Fear not, I am with you.
Is. 42:6	I, the LORD, have called you for the victory of justice, / I have grasped you by the hand, / I formed you, and set you / as a covenant of the people, / a light for the nations.
Is. 43:1	Fear not, for I have redeemed you; / I have called you by name; you are mine.
Is. 45:3	I will give you treasures out of the darkness, /and riches that have been hidden away, / That you may know that I am the Lord, / the God of Israel, who calls you by your name.

Is. 49:1	The LORD called me from birth, / from my mother's womb he gave me my name.
Is. 55:6	Seek the LORD while he may be found, / call him while he is near.
Is. 62:4	No more shall men call you "Forsaken," / or your land "Desolate," / But you shall be called "My Delight" / and your land "Espoused."
Is. 65:24	Before they call, I will answer; / while they are yet speaking, I will hearken to them.
Jer. 29:12	When you call me, when you go to pray to me, I will listen to you.
Jer. 33: 3	Call to me, and I will answer you; I will tell to you things great beyond reach of your knowledge.
Jonah 1:6	What are you doing asleep? Rise up, call upon your God!
Matt. 4:21-22	He called them, and immediately they left their boat and their father and followed him.
Matt. 5:9	Blessed are the peacemakers, / for they will be called children of God.
Matt. 9:13	Go and learn the meaning of the words, "I desire mercy, not sacrifice." I did not come to call the righteous but sinners.
Matt. 20:32	Jesus stopped and called them and said, "What do you want me to do for you?"
Mk. 10:49	"Take courage: get up, he is calling you."

Lk.1:48   For he has looked upon his handmaid's lowliness; / behold, from now on will all ages call me blessed.

Jo. 10:3   The gatekeeper opens it for him, and the sheep hear his voice, as he calls his own sheep by name and leads them out.

Jo. 15:15   I no longer call you slaves, because a slave does no know what his master is doing. I have called you friends because I have told you everything I have heard from my Father.

Acts 2:21   … and it shall be that everyone shall be saved who calls on the name of the Lord.

Acts 11:26   It was in Antioch that the disciples were first called Christians.

Rom.1:6-7   … among whom are you also, who are called to belong to Jesus Christ; to all the beloved of God in Rome, called to be holy.

Rom. 8:28   We know that all things work for good for those who love God, who are called according to his purpose.

Rom. 8:30   And those he predestined he also called; and those he called he also justified; and those he justified he also glorified.

Rom. 9:25   As indeed he says in Hosea: / "Those who were not my people, I will call 'my people,'/ and her who was not beloved I will call 'beloved' … "

Rom. 10:12   For there is no distinction between Jew and Greek; the same Lord is Lord of all, enriching all who call upon him.

1Cor. 1:2	… to you who have been sanctified in Christ Jesus, called to be holy, with all those everywhere who call upon the name of our Lord Jesus Christ …
1Cor. 1:9	God is faithful, and by him you were called to fellowship with his Son, Jesus Christ our Lord.
1Cor. 1:26-27	Consider your own calling, brothers. Not many of you were wise by human standards, not many were powerful, not many were of noble birth. Rather, God chose the foolish of the world to shame the wise, and God chose the weak of the world to shame the strong.
Gal. 1:15-16	But when [God], who from my mother's womb had set me apart and called me through his grace, was pleased to reveal his Son to me.
Gal. 5:13	For you were called for freedom, brothers. But do not use this freedom as an opportunity for the flesh; rather, serve one another through love.
Eph. 1:18	May the eyes of [your] hearts be enlightened, that you may know what is the hope that belongs to his call, what are the riches of glory in his inheritance among the holy ones.
Eph. 4:1-3	I, then, a prisoner for the Lord, urge you to live in a manner worthy of the call you have received, with all humility and gentleness, with patience, bearing with one another through love, striving to preserve the unity of the spirit through the bond of peace.
Eph. 4:4	One body and one Spirit, as you were also called to the one hope of your call.
Phil. 3:14	I continue my pursuit toward the goal, the prize of God's upward calling, in Christ Jesus.

Col. 3:15   And let the peace of Christ control your hearts, the peace into which you were also called in one body.

1Th. 2:12   ... exhorting and encouraging you and insisting that you conduct yourselves as worthy of the God who calls you into his kingdom and glory.

1Th. 5:23-24   May the God of peace himself make you perfectly holy and may you entirely, spirit, soul, and body, be preserved blameless for the coming of our Lord Jesus Christ. The one who calls you is faithful, and he will also accomplish it.

2Th. 1:11-12   We always pray for you, that our God may make you worthy of his calling and powerfully bring to fulfillment every good purpose and every effort of faith, that the name of our Lord Jesus may be glorified in you, and you in him.

1Tim. 6:12   Compete well for the faith. Lay hold of eternal life, to which you were called when you made the noble confession in the presence of many witnesses.

2Tim. 1:9   He saved us and called us to a holy life, not according to our works but according to his own design and the grace bestowed on us in Christ Jesus before time began.

2Tim.2:22   So turn from youthful desires and pursue righteousness, faith, love, and peace, along with those who call on the Lord with purity of heart.

1Pe. 1:15-16   As he who called you is holy, be holy yourselves in every aspect of your conduct, for it is written, "Be holy because I [am] holy."

1Pe. 2:9	But you are "a chosen race, a royal priesthood, a holy nation, a people of his own, so that you may announce the praises" of him who called you out of darkness into his wonderful light.
1Pe. 3:9	Do not return evil for evil, or insult for insult; but, on the contrary, a blessing, because to this you were called, that you might inherit a blessing.
2 Pe.1:10	Therefore, … be all the more eager to make your call and election firm, for, in doing so, you will never stumble.
1 Jo. 3:1	See what love the Father has bestowed on us that we may be called the children of God.
Jude1-2	To those who are called beloved in God the Father and kept safe for Jesus Christ: may mercy, peace, and love be yours in abundance.
Rev. 19:9	"Blessed are those who have been called to the wedding feast of the Lamb."

CHOSEN

When we honestly ask ourselves which person
in our lives means the most to us,
we often find that it is those who,
instead of giving much advise, solutions, or cures,
have chosen rather to share our pain
and touch our wounds with a gentle hand.

Henri Nouwen

CHOSEN

From my earliest recollections, the word chosen was more like ... NOT being chosen. Rather than being the pick of the crop, it was more like being one of the leftovers, when the kids were choosing teams! Like the character Ziggy, I could have my hand up 10 times to answer a question, but the teacher only chose me, for the question I did not know the correct answer. Being the eldest of six, it seemed that I was always chosen for the worst of chores. So *chosen* would not have been one of my favorite words; nor did it bring any great feelings. What a great surprise when, as an adult; I saw *chosen* in a new light, a sacred light, when chosen by God!

God chose ordinary people during ordinary times. Not at all what the world would choose. The Hebrew people must face this giant of a man in battle, and God chooses a very young David, a boy with a slingshot! In choosing prophets, God chose people who were the most unlikely. God chose Jeremiah, who complained that he was too young. Jonah, was chosen by God to go to the Ninevites, and he went the opposite direction. Amos was a shepherd and a dresser of sycamores when God chose him. Jesus comes upon the scene, and does He choose the knowledgeable temple people? No, Jesus chose ordinary fishermen and a tax collector. Earlier in my life, I did not connect with being chosen by God. I felt more like an accident, a disappointment, anything but ... "chosen."

Little by little, God broke through the veil of darkness that seemed to dictate, how I saw all things. John.15:16 echoes on in my heart,

It was not you who chose me, but I who chose you
and appointed you to go and bear fruit that will remain,
so that whatever you ask the Father in
my name he may give you.

When I heard that within the depth of my heart ... everything began to change! If I am good enough for God to choose me, then I must be okay. Then the questions:

Chosen for what?
What am I to do? To be?
What fruit can I bear?

Seeking the answers is a lifelong journey of self discovery in God's light and love!

Reflection Questions:

Do you know that God has chosen you? When did you realize this truth?
If not, what "veil of darkness" keeps you from this heart knowledge?
How does being chosen affect your life with God and others?

CHOSEN

Deut. 7:6	For you are a people sacred to the LORD, your God; he has chosen you from all nations on the face of the earth to be a people peculiarly his own.
Jos. 24:22	You are your own witnesses that you have chosen to serve the LORD.
2 Chr.7:16	And now I have chosen and consecrated this house that my name may be there forever; my eyes and my heart also shall be there always.
Ps. 33:12	Happy the nation whose God is the LORD, / the people chosen as his very own.
Ps. 65:5	Happy the chosen ones you bring / to dwell in your courts. / May we be filled with the good things of your house, / the blessings of your holy temple!
Ps. 89:3-4	"My love is established forever; / my loyalty will stand as long as the heavens. / "I have made a covenant with my chosen one."
Ps. 89:21	"I have chosen David, my servant; / with my holy oil I have anointed him."
Ps. 105:43	He brought his people out with joy, / his chosen ones with shouts of triumph.
Ps. 106:5	That I may see the prosperity of your chosen, / rejoice in the joy of your people, / and glory with your heritage.
Ps. 119: 30	The way of loyalty I have chosen; / I have set your edicts before me.

Ps. 119: 173   Keep your hand ready to help me, / for I have chosen your precepts.

Ps. 132: 13   Yes, the LORD has chosen Zion, / desired it for a dwelling.

Ps. 135: 4   For the LORD has chosen Jacob, / Israel as a treasured possession.

Is. 41:8-10   But you, ... Jacob, whom I have chosen, / ... You whom I have called my servant, / whom I have chosen and will not cast off - / Fear not, I am with you!

Is. 43:10   You are my witnesses, says the LORD, / my servants whom I have chosen / To know and believe in me / and understand that it is I.

Is. 44:1-2   Hear then, O Jacob, my servant, / Israel, whom I have chosen. / Thus says the LORD who made you, / your help, who formed you from the womb: / Fear not, O Jacob, my servant, / the darling whom I have chosen.

Is. 45:4   For the sake of Jacob, my servant, / of Israel my chosen one, / I have called you by your name.

Matt. 12:18   "Behold, my servant whom I have chosen, / my beloved in whom I delight; / I shall place my spirit upon him, / and he will proclaim justice to the Gentiles."

Matt. 22:14   Many are invited, but few are chosen.

Lk. 9:35   Then from the cloud came a voice that said, "This is my chosen Son, listen to him."

Lk. 10:42   There is need of only one thing. Mary has chosen the better part and it will not be taken from her.

Jn. 15:16   It was not you who chose me, but I chose you and appointed you to go and bear fruit that will remain, so that whatever you ask the Father in my name he may give you.

Jn. 15:19 If you belonged to the world, the world would love its own; but because you do not belong to the world, and I have chosen you out of the world, the world hates you.

1Cor. 1:27 Rather, God chose the foolish of the world to shame the wise, and God chose the weak of the world to shame the strong.

Eph. 1:3-4 Blessed be the God and Father of our Lord Jesus Christ, who has blessed us in Christ with every spiritual blessing in the heavens, as he chose us in him, before the foundation of the world, to be holy and without blemish before him.

Col. 3:12 Put on then, as God's chosen ones, holy and beloved, heartfelt compassion, kindness, humility, gentleness, and patience.

2Th. 2:13 But we ought to give thanks to God for you always, brothers loved by the Lord, because God chose you as the firstfruits for salvation through sanctification by the Spirit and belief in truth.

2Tim. 2:10 Therefore, I bear with everything for the sake of those who are chosen, so that they too may obtain the salvation that is in Christ Jesus, together with eternal glory.

1Pe. 2:4 Come to him, a living stone, rejected by human beings but chosen and precious in the sight of God.

1Pe. 2:9 But you are "a chosen race, a royal priesthood, a holy nation, a people of his own, so that you may announce the praises" of him who called you out of darkness into his wonderful light.

COURAGE

I learned that courage was not the absence of fear,
but the triumph over it.
The brave man is not he who does not feel afraid,
but he who conquers that fear!

Nelson Mandela

COURAGE

When I was little, I used to think that one needed courage to fight wild animals and to ride roller coasters. I didn't find that courage within myself. Actually, I have felt that I am basically wimpy and fearful of so much. I read a book by Hannah Hurnard called <u>Hinds Feet on High Places</u>. The main character and I had a lot in common, her name was Much AFRAID.

"Afraid of what," you might ask? I am fearful of the normal things girls are afraid of ... snakes, bugs and loud noises. On a more personal level I would have to add: fear of rejection, change, failure, of being judged harshly, and not being good enough. So what does the word "courage" offer to me?

It truly was in the words of Jesus that I began to find my courage. As I took in the strength of the gospel message and answered the call to discipleship, I realized that my courage comes from the Lord. Choosing to be a "fool for Christ," I stepped out in faith and have been amazed at what God has done through me.

The hardest thing for me to do, was to have the courage to see myself truthfully as God sees me. That journey of self discovery is perhaps the most difficult journey of all. Yet, each day I open myself to God and ask for the courage to do just that ... to see myself honestly. Then I need to accept myself, as human and a work still in progress.

When I think of courage, I think of Peter when he stepped out of the boat to walk on water. I want to learn to walk on water, so to speak, and I know that is a lifelong journey of faith! But when I see those battling cancer ... with joy, or that person who fights for justice so that her neighborhood can be safe, or a woman bent with arthritis still taking care of an elderly parent ... well, I know I have seen present day "water walkers!" I am encouraged! Just keep your eyes on Jesus!

Patti King

Reflection Questions:

What does courage mean in your life?

What do you need courage for?

Where do you draw your courage from?

Courage

2Sam. 7:27 Therefore your servant now finds the courage to make this prayer to you.

Tobit 5:10 Take courage! God has healing in store for you, so take courage!

Tobit 7:17 Be brave, my daughter. May the Lord of heaven grant you joy in place of your grief. Courage, my daughter.

Judith 11:1 Take courage, lady; have no fear in your heart!

Esther C:23 Be mindful of us, O Lord. Manifest yourself in the time of our distress and give me courage.

Ps. 23:4 Even when I walk through a dark valley, / I fear no harm for you are at my side, / your rod and staff give me courage.

Ps. 27:14 Wait for the Lord, take courage; / be stouthearted, wait for the Lord!

Sir. 30:23 Distract yourself, renew your courage, / drive resentment far away from you.

Sir. 34:13 Lively is the courage of those who fear the Lord, / for they put their hope in their savior.

Is. 12:2 God indeed is my savior; / I am confident and unafraid. / My strength and my courage is the Lord, / and he has been my savior!

Dan. 10:19 Fear not, beloved, you are safe; take courage and be strong.

Matt. 9:2   When Jesus saw their faith, he said to the paralytic, "Courage, child, your sins are forgiven."

Matt. 14:27   At once [Jesus] spoke to them, "Take courage, it is I; do not be afraid."

Mk. 10:48-52 But he kept calling out, " Son of David, have pity on me." Jesus stopped and said, "Call him." So they called the blind man, saying to him, "Take courage: get up, he is calling you."

Jn. 16:33   I have told you this so that you might have peace in me. In the world you will have trouble, but take courage, I have conquered the world.

1Cor. 16:13-14 Be on your guard, stand firm in the faith, be courageous, be strong. Your every act should be done in love.

Eph. 6:18-20 With all prayer and supplication, pray at every opportunity in the Spirit. To that end be watchful with all perseverance and supplication for all the holy ones and also for me, that speech may be given me to open my mouth, to make known with boldness the mystery of the gospel for which I am an ambassador in chains, so that I may have the courage to speak as I must.

1Thess. 2:2 After we had suffered and been insolently treated, as you know, in Philippi, we drew courage through our God to speak to you the gospel of God with much struggle.

DELIGHT

One all possessing love I ask
my God, my soul centered in You,
making a delightful nest,
a resting place most pleasing.

Teresa of Avila

DELIGHT

Listening to the news, weighed down with worries and fears, we may find trouble remembering what the word "delight" means. So let us brainstorm what delight brings to mind:

a giggling baby playing in a bathtub,

children running through the sprinkler on a hot day,

the aroma of fresh baked bread,

the surprise of a hot air balloon rising in front of you,

first time on a Ferris wheel,

seeing your beloved coming toward you,

Christmas morning,

and there is so much more. Children can teach us so much about delight! Just watch a child take delight in a chasing a butterfly, or playing in a mud puddle! What is it we have long forgotten since we were little? What blocks our ability to "delight" in anything?

In Isaiah 62:4, God says,

... But you shall be called "My Delight."

How can this be? Can we believe that we are God's "delight?" One of my favorite people to watch on TV was Lucy, on I LOVE LUCY. Each week we would look forward to seeing what kind of a mess Lucy was getting herself into and how she was going to get out of it. We would giggle with delight at her antics. I am more like Lucy than any saint. Before God answers the prayer that I will surely call out, God is probably laughing in sheer delight at my antics! Perhaps we take ourselves way too seriously!

We are God's creation, each one different, precious, and delightful. Can I take delight in God? Do I take the time to delight in others? Do I even know how to live with delight? Perhaps, our prayer should be:

Lord, nurture my inner child that I may live as Your Delight!

Reflection Questions:

What does the word delight mean to you?

God takes great delight in you. How does that make you feel?

What needs to change in you that you might dwell in "delight" more often?

DELIGHT

Deut. 30:9 Then the LORD, your God, will increase in more than goodly measure the returns from all your labors, ... for the Lord, your God, will again take delight in your prosperity.

Job 22:26-27 For then you shall delight in the Almighty / and you shall lift up your face toward God. / You shall entreat him and he will hear you, / and your vows you shall fulfill.

Ps. 9:3 I will delight and rejoice in you; / I will sing hymns to your name, Most High.

Ps. 16:11 You will show me the path to life, / abounding joy in your presence, / the delights at your right hand forever.

Ps. 35:27 Exalted be the LORD / who delights in the peace of his loyal servant.

Ps. 36:8-9 How precious is your love, O God! / We take refuge in the shadow of your wings. / We feast on the rich food of your house; / from your delightful stream you give us drink.

Ps. 37:4 Find your delight in the LORD / who will give you your heart's desire!

Ps. 37:11 But the poor will possess the land, / will delight in great prosperity.

Ps. 40:9 To do your will is my delight; / my God, your law is in my heart!

Ps. 43:4 That I may come to the altar of God, / to God, my joy, my delight.

Ps. 111:2 Great are the works of the LORD, / to be treasured for all their delights.

Ps. 119:16 In your laws I take delight; / I will never forget your word.

Ps.119:24 Your decrees are my delight; / they are my counselors.

Ps. 119:35 Lead me in the path of your commands, / for that is my delight.

Ps. 119:47 I delight in your commands, / which I dearly love.

Ps. 119:77 Show me compassion that I may live, / for your teaching is my delight.

Ps. 119:174 I long for your salvation, LORD; / your teaching is my delight.

Ps. 149:4 For the LORD takes delight in his people, / honors the poor with victory.

Pro. 8:30 Then I was beside him as his craftsman, / and I was his delight day by day.

Pro. 11:20 Those who walk blamelessly are his delight.

Pro. 15:8 The prayer of the upright is his delight.

Pro. 16:13 The king takes delight in honest lips, / and the man who speaks what is right he loves.

Pro. 29:17 Correct your son, and he will bring you comfort, / and give delight to your soul.

So. 2:3	As an apple tree among the trees of the woods, / so is my lover among men. / I delight to rest in his shadow.
So. 5:16	His mouth is sweetness itself; / he is all delight. / Such is my lover, and such my friend.
So. 7:7	How beautiful you are, how pleasing, / my love, my delight!
Sir. 25:1	With three things I am delighted, / for they are pleasing to the LORD and to men: / Harmony among brethren, friendship among neighbors, /and the mutual love of husband and wife.
Is. 11:2-3	The spirit of the LORD shall rest upon him: / a spirit of wisdom and of understanding, / A spirit of counsel and of strength, / a spirit of knowledge and of fear of the Lord, / and his delight shall be the fear of the Lord.
Is. 55:2	Why spend your money for what is not bread; / your wages for what fails to satisfy? / Heed me, and you shall eat well, / you shall delight in rich fare.
Is. 62:4	No more shall men call you "Forsaken," / or your land "Desolate,"/ But you shall be called "My Delight," / and your land "Espoused," / For the Lord delights in you!
Is. 65:18	Instead there shall always be rejoicing and happiness / in what I create; / For I create Jerusalem to be a joy / and its people to be a delight.

Jer. 32:40-41   I will make with them an eternal covenant, never to cease doing good to them; into their hearts I will put the fear of me, that they may never depart from me I will take delight in doing good to them; I will replant them firmly in this land, with all my heart and soul.

Hos. 6:6   For it is love that I desire, not sacrifice, / and knowledge of God rather than holocausts.

Matt. 12:18   "Behold my servant, whom I have chosen, / my beloved in whom I delight."

Rom. 7:22   For I take delight in the law of God, in my inner self.

DWELL

To dwell with You,
Lord,
is all I ask;
it matters not where!

Patti King

DWELL

I love the word dwell! We can live anywhere; but to dwell is a choice of the heart! When I think of dwell, I imagine a dove settling into it's nest, carefully chosen, purposely placed. As a child, I always dreamed of living in that precious cottage with the white picket fence, where happiness dwelled. What I discovered is that it isn't what you live in; or where you live; but who you dwell with that matters.

From my earliest memories, I believed that God dwelled in the church where the soft darkness was broken by the candlelight, that glowed a sacred red. As I grew, my understanding of where God dwells was greatly expanded! Nature opened my eyes to see God dwelling with all of creation. Mountaintops, seashores, quiet lakes and country roads, God could be found every place! If only I stop and become aware of that moment, I can feel God's presence!

But the surprise of my heart, was the day I truly awakened to the understanding that my God chooses to dwell within me! I am the temple of the holy Spirit! I have come to understand that God desires to dwell within me, and that makes all the difference to my life. But that truth also challenges me to live in a manner worthy of God's presence. God dwells with all creation, all people, and that calls forth from me an attitude of respect and reverence for all.

So if our paths cross, do not be surprised if I say, "The spirit in me, rejoices with the spirit in you!" Those who "dwell" with God can sense the indwelling presence of Love!

Reflection Questions:

Where and with whom do you choose to dwell?

How do you feel about God's choosing to dwell with you?

In the awareness that God dwells with you, what difference does that make in how you live? interact with others? with God?

DWELL

Lev. 8:10   Taking the anointing oil, Moses anointed and consecrated the Dwelling, with all that was in it.

1Ki. 8:30   Listen to the petitions of your servant and of your people Israel which they offer in this place. Listen from your heavenly dwelling and grant pardon.

Job 38:19   Which is the way to the dwelling place of light?

Ps. 15:1-2   LORD, who may abide in your tent? / Who may dwell on your holy mountain? / Whoever walks without blame, / doing what is right.

Ps. 16: 8-9   I keep the LORD always before me; / with the Lord at my right, I shall never be shaken. / Therefore my heart is glad, my soul rejoices; / my body also dwells secure.

Ps. 23:6   Only goodness and love will pursue me / all the days of my life; / I will dwell in the house of the Lord / for years to come.

Ps. 26:8   LORD, I love the house where you dwell, / the tenting-place of your glory.

Ps. 27:4   One thing I ask of the LORD; / this I seek: / To dwell in the LORD' s house / all the days of my life.

Ps. 37:3   Trust in the LORD and do good / that you may dwell in the land and live secure.

Ps. 43:3   Send your light and fidelity, / that they may be my guide. / And bring me to your holy mountain, / to the place of your dwelling.

Ps. 46:5	Streams of the river gladden the city of God, / the holy dwelling of the Most High.
Ps. 61:5	Then I will ever dwell in your tent, / take refuge in the shelter of your wings.
Ps. 65:5	Happy the chosen ones you bring / to dwell in your courts. / May we be filled with the good things of your house, / the blessings of your holy temple!
Ps. 84:2-3	How lovely your dwelling, / O LORD of hosts! / My soul yearns and pines / for the courts of the Lord.
Ps. 84:5	Happy are those who dwell in your house! / They never cease to praise you.
Ps. 91:1-2	You who dwell in the shelter of the Most High, / who abide in the shadow of the Almighty. / Say to the Lord, "My refuge and fortress, / my God in whom I trust."
Ps. 132:13-14	Yes, the LORD has chosen Zion, / desired it for a dwelling: / "This is my resting place forever; / here I will dwell, for I desire it."
Ps. 133:1	How good it is, how pleasant, / where the people dwell as one!
Ps. 140:13-14	For I know the LORD will secure / justice for the needy, their rights for the poor. / Then the just will give thanks to your name; / the upright will dwell in your presence.
Pro. 1:33	But he who obeys me dwells in security / in peace, without fear of harm.

Ecc. 5:19	For he will hardly dwell on the shortness of his life, because God lets him busy himself with the joy of his heart.
Wis. 7:27-28	And passing into holy souls from age to age, / she produces friends of God and prophets. / For there is nought God loves, be it not one who dwells with Wisdom.
Sir. 4:13	He who holds her [wisdom] fast inherits glory; / wherever he dwells, the LORD bestows blessings.
Is. 30:19	O people of Zion, who dwell in Jerusalem, / no more will you weep; / He will be gracious to you when you cry out, / as soon as he hears he will answer you.
Is. 32:18	My people will live in peaceful country, / in secure dwellings and quiet resting places.
Is. 57:15	On high I dwell, and in holiness, / and with the crushed and dejected in spirit, / To revive the spirits of the dejected, / to revive the hearts of the crushed.
Ez. 37:27-28	My dwelling shall be with them; I will be their God, and they shall be my people. Thus the nations shall know that it is I, the Lord, who make Israel holy, when my sanctuary shall be set up among them forever.
Zech. 2:17	Silence, all mankind, in the presence of the LORD! for he stirs forth from his holy dwelling.
Acts 2:26	Therefore my heart has been glad and my tongue has exulted; / my flesh, too, will dwell in hope.
Rom.8:9	But you are not in the flesh; on the contrary, you are in the spirit, if only the Spirit of God dwells in you.

2Cor.12:9   He said to me: "My grace is sufficient for you, for power is made perfect in weakness." I will rather boast most gladly of my weaknesses, in order that the power of Christ may dwell with me.

Eph. 2:22   In him you also are being built together into a dwelling place of God in the Spirit.

Eph. 3:17-19   That Christ may dwell in your hearts through faith; that you, rooted and grounded in love, may have strength to comprehend with all the holy ones what is the breadth and length and height and depth, and to know the love of Christ that surpasses knowledge, so that you may be filled with all the fullness of God.

Col. 3:16   Let the word of Christ dwell in you richly.

2Tim. 1:14   Guard this rich trust with the help of the holy Spirit that dwells within us.

Rev. 21:3   I heard a loud voice from the throne saying, "Behold, God's dwelling is with the human race. He will dwell with them and they will be his people and God himself will always be with them [as their God]."

FAITH

When I took the leap,
I had faith I would find a net,
instead I learned I could fly.

John Calvi

FAITH

I heard a long time ago that faith isn't faith until you have nothing to hang on to. This is illustrated so beautifully in the story of the man who falls off a cliff. The only thing that keeps him from falling to the earth is hanging on to a branch. He calls out to God for HELP. God answers, "Let go!" He responds, "Is there anyone else up there?"

Do we live as persons of faith? We storm the gates of heaven with prayers for rain; but how many of us bring an umbrella? As Christians, we say that we believe in life after death … but do we really? I believe we doubt more than we believe.

It occurred to me why Jesus chose so many fishermen to follow him, fishermen are people who live faith. They have faith that if they show up prepared to catch fish, they will. And they will stay patiently and wait for hours! My husband always makes me smile when he gets ready to go fishing at the coast. He hauls out this huge ice chest and fills it with ice for the fish he is "going to catch." Sometimes he fills it with fish … most of the time he doesn't. But he continues to fill the ice chest with ice. Now that is faith!

I want to have faith like a trapeze artist who literally lets go, to fly through the air assured that their partner will catch them! Hopefully, I have been that for my children and grandchildren, that solid person who is there to catch them no matter what! God is like the trapeze partner, who waits for us to let go. So why do we hesitate? What does it take for our faith to grow past the doubts and trust God?

Life gives us so many opportunities to experience this gracious gift of God, perhaps it is time to "swing out and let go." Have a little faith!

Reflection Questions:

When is a time that you truly had to live in faith?

What did this time teach you about yourself? about God?

Who has faith in you?

FAITH

Ps. 13:6	I trust in your faithfulness. / Grant my heart joy in your help, / That I may sing of the Lord, / "How good our God has been to me."
Ps. 25:10	All the paths of the LORD are faithful love / toward those who honor the covenant demands.
Ps. 26:3	Your love is before my eyes; / I walk guided by your faithfulness.
Ps. 31:6	Into your hands I commend my spirit; / you will redeem me, LORD, faithful God.
Ps. 42:9	At dawn may the LORD bestow faithful love / that I may sing praise through the night.
Ps. 52:10	But, I, like an olive tree in the house of God, / trust in God's faithful love forever.
Ps. 57:11	Your love towers to the heavens; / your faithfulness to the skies.
Ps. 85:9	I will listen for the word of God; / surely the LORD will proclaim peace / To his people, to the faithful, / to those who trust in him.
Ps. 117:2	The LORD's love for us is strong; / the LORD is faithful forever. / Hallelujah!
Wis. 3:9	Those who trust in him shall understand truth, / and the faithful shall abide with him in love.
Sir. 6:14	A faithful friend is a sturdy shelter; / he who finds one finds a treasure.

Sir. 6:15	A faithful friend is beyond price, / no sum can balance his worth.
Sir. 39:13	Listen, my faithful children: open up your petals, / like roses planted near running waters.
Matt. 9:22	"Courage, daughter! Your faith has saved you."
Matt. 9:28-30	"Do you believe that I can do this?" "Yes, Lord," they said to him. Then he touched their eyes and said, "Let it be done for you according to your faith." And their eyes were opened.
Matt. 15:28	Then Jesus said to her in reply, "O woman, great is your faith! Let it be done for you as you wish."
Matt. 17:20	"Amen, I say to you, if you have faith the size of a mustard seed, you will say to this mountain, 'Move from here to there,' and it will move. Nothing will be impossible for you."
Matt. 21:22	Whatever you ask for in prayer with faith, you will receive.
Matt. 25:23	Well done, my good and faithful servant. Since you were faithful in small matters, I will give you great responsibilities. Come share your master's joy.
Mk. 5:34	He said to her, "Daughter, your faith has saved you. Go in peace and be cured of your affliction."
Mk. 5:36	"Do not be afraid; just have faith."
Mk. 10: 52	"Go your way; your faith has saved you."
Mk. 11:22, 24	Jesus said to them in reply, "Have faith in God. Therefore, I tell you, all that you ask for in prayer, believe that you will receive it and it shall be yours."

Lk. 7:50	But he said to the woman, "Your faith has saved you; go in peace."
Lk. 17:5	And the apostles said to the Lord, "Increase our faith." The Lord replied, "If you have faith the size of a mustard seed, you would say to [this] mulberry tree, 'Be uprooted and planted in the sea,' and it would obey you."
Lk. 17:19	"Stand up and go; your faith has saved you."
Jn. 14:1	"Do not let your hearts be troubled. You have faith in God; have faith also in me."
Rom. 5:1	Therefore, since we have been justified by faith, we have peace with God through our Lord Jesus Christ.
1Cor. 1:9	God is faithful, and by him you were called to fellowship with his Son, Jesus Christ, our Lord.
1Cor. 2:5	… so that your faith might rest not on human wisdom but on the power of God.
1Cor. 10:13	No trial has come to you but what is human. God is faithful and will not let you be tried beyond your strength; but with the trial he will also provide a way out, so that you may be able to bear it.
1Cor. 13:2	And if I have the gift of prophecy and comprehend all mysteries and all knowledge; if I have all faith so as to move mountains, but do not have love, I am nothing.
1Cor. 16:13-14	Be on your guard, stand firm in the faith, be courageous, be strong. Your every act should be done with love.
2Cor. 5:7	We walk by faith, not by sight.

2Cor. 13:5   Examine yourselves to see whether you are living in faith. Test yourselves. Do you not realize that Jesus Christ is in you?

Gal. 2:20   ... yet I live, no longer I, but Christ lives in me; insofar as I now live in the flesh. I live by faith in the Son of God who has loved me and given himself up for me.

Gal. 5:5   For through the Spirit, by faith, we await the hope of righteousness.

Gal. 5:22-23   The fruit of the Spirit is love, joy, peace, patience, kindness, generosity, faithfulness, gentleness, self-control.

Eph. 1:15-16   I too, hearing of your faith in the Lord Jesus and of your love for all the holy ones, do not cease giving thanks for you.

Eph. 2:8   For by grace you have been saved through faith, and this is not from you; it is a gift of God.

Eph. 3:16-17   ... that he may grant you in accord with the riches of his glory to be strengthened with power through his Spirit in the inner self, and that Christ may dwell in your hearts through faith.

Eph. 4:4b-6   You were also called to the one hope of your call; one Lord, one faith, one baptism; one God and Father of all, who is over all and through all and in all.

Eph. 6:16   In all circumstances, hold faith as a shield, to quench all [the] flaming arrows of the evil one.

Col. 1:3-4   We always give thanks to God, the Father of our Lord Jesus Christ, when we pray for you, for we have heard of your faith in Christ Jesus and the love you have for all the holy ones.

Col. 1:22-23 … he has now reconciled in his fleshly body through his death, to present you holy, without blemish, and irreproachable before him, provided that you persevere in the faith, firmly grounded, stable, and not shifting from the hope of the gospel that you heard.

Col. 2:6-7 So as you received Christ Jesus the Lord, walk in him, rooted in him and built upon him and established in the faith as you were taught, abounding in thanksgiving.

Col. 2:12 You were buried with him in baptism, in which you were also raised with him through faith in the power of God, who raised him from the dead.

1 Thess. 1:2-4 We give thanks to God always for all of you, remembering you in our prayers, unceasingly calling to mind your work of faith and labor of love and endurance in hope of our Lord Jesus Christ.

1 Thess. 5:8 Since we are of the day, let us be sober, putting on the breastplate of faith and love and the helmet that is hope for salvation.

2 Thess. 1:3 We ought to thank God always for you, as is fitting, because your faith flourishes ever more, and the love of every one of you for one another grows ever greater.

2 Thess. 1:4 We ourselves boast of you in the churches of God regarding your endurance and faith in all your persecutions and the afflictions you endure.

2 Thess. 1:11-12 We always pray for you, that our God may make you worthy of his calling and powerfully bring to fulfillment every good purpose and every effort of faith, that the name of our Lord Jesus may be glorified in you, and you in him, in accord with the grace of our God and Lord Jesus Christ.

1Tim. 1:2 … to Timothy, my true child in faith: grace, mercy, and peace from God the Father and Christ Jesus our Lord.

1Tim. 1:5 The aim of this instruction is love from a pure heart, a good conscience, and a sincere faith.

1Tim. 2:15 … women persevere in faith and love and holiness, with self-control.

1Tim. 4:12 Let no one have contempt for your youth, but set an example for those who believe, in speech, conduct, love, faith, and purity.

1Tim. 6:11-12 Pursue righteousness, devotion, faith, love, patience and gentleness. Compete well for the faith.

2Tim. 4:7 I have competed well; I have finished the race; I have kept the faith.

Philemon 4-5 I give thanks to my God always, remembering you in my prayers, as I hear of the love and faith you have in the Lord Jesus and for all the holy ones.

Heb. 11:1 Faith is the realization of what is hoped for and evidence of things not seen.

Ja. 1:2-3 Consider it all joy, when you encounter various trials, for you know that the testing of your faith produces perseverance.

Ja. 2:26 For just as a body without a spirit is dead, so also faith without works is dead.

Ja. 5:14-15   Is anyone among you sick? He should summon the presbyters of the church, and they should pray over him and anoint [him] with oil in the name of the Lord, and the prayer of faith will save the sick person, and the Lord will raise him up.

3Jn. 5   Beloved, you are faithful in all you do.

Jude 20-21   But you beloved, build yourselves up in your most holy faith; pray in the holy Spirit. Keep yourselves in the love of God and wait for the mercy of our Lord Jesus Christ that leads to eternal life.

Rev. 2:10   Remain faithful until death, and I will give you the crown of life.

FORGIVENESS

Those who cannot forgive others
break the bridge over which
they themselves must pass.

Confucius

FORGIVENESS

Forgiveness, is an act of love! Before I look at how I forgive, I need to look at how God has forgiven me. As hard hearted and sinful as I have been, how can God forgive me? Yet I see what merciful grace God has showered me with throughout my life. God has forgiven me for my sins and my failure to love. I am humbled. Throughout my human life, it has been ... I will love you if, ... I will forgive you if; but not with God. God simply, totally loves, forgives and calls me His own! If we really understood that, wouldn't we want to go out and simply forgive all?

Lord, why is this so hard? Why do we want to hold on to grudges and keep a stance that seems to give us power over one another? Why can't we simply love as you love?

True healing comes from forgiving others; and most especially myself! I have experienced this great truth! Never did I realize how much I held myself in bondage, by not forgiving myself. I evidently forgot that I am human and had expected myself to be perfect. Interesting, as I forgave myself, how much easier it was to forgive others. In forgiving all, I emptied myself so much that God could fill the void ... and God did. God brought healing to my life, filling me with such great peace, like sitting at the beach and letting grace just wash over me.

Not forgiving is like a great barrier wall that keeps out the sunshine. It isn't that God is not there, for God is; but we put up the blockages that keep us from realizing God's presence! Forgiveness is a great key to inner freedom! I have the key and so do you!

Reflection Questions:

Take time to reflect on God's forgiveness in your life.

Are there any blockages you need to tear down (forgive) so that you might realize the presence of God's healing love?

Patti King

Who most needs your forgiveness right now?

What do you need to forgive yourself for? Give yourself the gift of forgiveness!

FORGIVENESS

1Ki. 8:36   Listen in heaven and forgive the sin of your servant and of your people Israel, teaching them the right way to live and sending rain upon this land of yours which you have given to your people as their heritage.

1Ki. 8:38-39   If then any one … has remorse of conscience and offers some prayer or petition, stretching out his hands toward this temple, listen from your heavenly dwelling place and forgive.

Ps. 32:1   Happy the sinner whose fault is removed, / whose sin is forgiven.

Ps. 86: 5   Lord, you are kind and forgiving, / most loving to all who call on you.

Ps. 130:4   But with you is forgiveness / and so you are revered.

Sir. 2:11   Compassionate and merciful is the LORD; / he forgives sins, he saves in time of trouble.

Sir. 17:24   How great the mercy of the LORD, / his forgiveness of those who return to him!

Sir. 28:2   Forgive your neighbor's injustice; / then when you pray, your own sins will be forgiven.

Jer. 31:34   No longer will they have need to teach their friends and kinsmen how to know the Lord. All, from least to greatest shall know me, says the Lord, for I will forgive their evildoing and remember their sin no more.

Matt. 6:12   … and forgive us our debts, / as we forgive our debtors.

Matt. 6:14   If you forgive others their transgressions, your heavenly Father will forgive you.

Matt. 9:5   Which is easier to say, "Your sins are forgiven," or to say, "Rise and walk?"

Matt. 12:31-32 Therefore, I say to you, every sin and blasphemy will be forgiven people, but blasphemy against the Spirit will not be forgiven. And whoever speaks a word against the Son of Man will be forgiven; but whoever speaks against the holy Spirit will not be forgiven, either in this age or in the age to come.

Matt. 18:21   Lord, if my brother sins against me, how often must I forgive him? As many as seven times?

Matt. 18:35   So will my heavenly Father do to you, unless each of you forgives his brother from his heart.

Matt. 26:28   … for this is my blood of the covenant, which will be shed on behalf of many for the forgiveness of sins.

Mk. 2:5   When Jesus saw their faith, he said to the paralytic, "Child, your sins are forgiven."

Mk. 11:25   When you stand to pray, forgive anyone against whom you have a grievance, so that your heavenly Father may in turn forgive you your transgressions

Lk. 1:77   … to give his people knowledge of salvation / through the forgiveness of their sins.

Lk. 7:47   So I tell you, her many sins have been forgiven; hence, she has shown great love. But the one to whom little is forgiven, loves little.

Lk. 11:4	… and forgive us our sins / for we ourselves forgive everyone in debt to us.
Lk. 17:3	Be on your guard! If your brother sins, rebuke him; and if he repents, forgive him.
Lk. 17:4	And if he wrongs you seven times in one day and returns to you seven times saying, "I am sorry," you should forgive him.
Lk. 23:34	Father, forgive them, they know not what they are doing.
Jn. 20:23	Whose sins you forgive are forgiven them, and whose sins you retain are retained.
Acts 2:38	Repent and be baptized, every one of you, in the name of Jesus Christ for the forgiveness of your sins; and you will receive the gift of the holy Spirit.
Acts 10:43	To him all the prophets bear witness, that everyone who believes in him will receive forgiveness of sins through his name.
Acts 26:18	… to open their eyes that they may turn from darkness to light and from the power of Satan to God, so that they may obtain forgiveness of sins and an inheritance among those who have been consecrated by faith in me.
Rom. 4:7	Blessed are they whose iniquities are forgiven / and whose sins are covered.
2Cor. 2:7-8	… so that on the contrary you should forgive and encourage him instead, or else the person may be overwhelmed by excessive pain. Therefore, I urge you to reaffirm your love for him.

Eph. 1:7-8   In him we have redemption by his blood, the forgiveness of transgressions, in accord with the riches of his grace, that he lavished upon us.

Eph. 4:32   Be kind to one another, compassionate, forgiving one another as God has forgiven you in Christ.

Col.1:13-14   He delivered us from the power of darkness and transferred us to the kingdom of his beloved Son, in whom we have redemption, the forgiveness of sins.

Col. 3:13   … bearing with one another and forgiving one another, if one has a grievance against another; as the Lord has forgiven you, so must you also do.

Ja. 5:15   … and the prayer of faith will save the sick person, and the Lord will raise him up. If he has committed any sins, he will be forgiven.

1Jn. 1:9   If we acknowledge our sins, he is faithful and just and will forgive our sins and cleanse us from every wrongdoing.

GIFT

The most precious gift
we can offer others is our presence.
When mindfulness embraces those we love,
they will bloom like flowers.

Thich Nhat Hanh

GIFT

What child, young or old, would not get excited at the prospect of opening a gift? None that I know. "Gift" is a word that brings joyful anticipation to the one who is to receive it. So what gifts has God given to us? The first time I heard this question in my twenties I thought ... hmm ... beauty? ... not really. Intelligence? ... maybe some. Riches? ... certainly not. Only later through the years did I truly discover my gifts. Life, salvation, faith, joy, peace, faithful friends, family, love, a creative spirit, and the list goes on and on. Because we are looking for certain gifts, we miss the abundance that God has given to us.

For instance, look at a field of flowers. Like a "zoom in camera," zoom in on one flower. Study all of it's characteristics that make it unique and beautiful ... its color, its aroma, its shape. It has been there all along and yet we have passed it by countless times. Now think of all the ways that this flower is a gift to the butterflies and bugs. It's beauty is a gift to the whole world. Next time, perhaps we should really stop and smell the flowers!

One of these precious gifts is You and Me! Although God created the gift, we package ourselves as how we want others to see us. We tend to hide the real gift of ourselves. Why? Perhaps fear of rejection keeps us from showing our true selves. Only those who dare to go deeper through the layers will discover the treasure hidden beneath. Many of us have been wrapped so tightly, and for so long, that we too may have forgotten our own giftedness.

So what is our response to our generous gift-giving God?

God, the Giver of all Good Gifts, gives us life, love, each other,
gifts of the Spirit, natural wonders, and so much more!
    1. Am I open to receive these gifts?
    2. What do I do with them?
        * Do I leave them unopened?

       * Do I put them on a shelf, to collect dust?
       * Do I readily use these gifts?
       * Do I reject them?
3. Do I thank God for these gifts?
4. Do I treat others as a gift from God?

Reflection Questions:

You are a gift from God. Celebrate it! Make a list of the gifts God has given you. (Ask others what they see as your gifts.) How do you use the gifts God gave you?

GIFT

Ps. 103:2-3   Bless the LORD, my soul; / do not forget all the gifts of God, / Who pardons all your sins, / heals all your ills.

Ps. 127:3   Children too are a gift from the LORD, / the fruit of the womb, a reward.

Ecc. 3:13   For every man, moreover, to eat and drink and enjoy the fruit of all his labor is a gift of God.

Wis. 8:21   And knowing that I could not otherwise possess her except God gave it— / and this, too, was prudence, to know whose is the gift-- / I went to the Lord and besought him.

Sir. 3:17   Conduct your affairs with humility, / and you will be loved more than a giver of gifts.

Sir. 11:17   The LORD's gift remains with the just; / his favor brings continued success.

Sir. 26: 3   A good wife is a generous gift / bestowed upon him who fears the LORD.

Matt. 5:23   Therefore, if you bring your gift to the altar, and there recall that your brother has anything against you, leave your gift there at the altar, go first and be reconciled with your brother, and then come and offer your gift.

Matt. 7:11   If you then, who are wicked, know how to give good gifts to your children, how much more will your heavenly Father give good things to those who ask him.

Jn. 4:10	If you knew the gift of God and who is saying to you, "Give me a drink," you would have asked him and he would have given you living water.
Jn. 17:24	Father, they are your gift to me. I wish that where I am they also may be with me.
Acts 2:38	Repent and be baptized, every one of you, in the name of Jesus Christ for the forgiveness of your sins; and you will receive the gift of the holy Spirit.
Rom. 1:11	For I long to see you, that I may share with you some spiritual gift so that you may be strengthened.
Rom. 6:23	For the wages of sin is death, but the gift of God is eternal life in Christ Jesus our Lord.
Rom. 11:29	For the gifts and the call of God are irrevocable.
Rom. 12: 6-8	Since we have gifts that differ according to the grace given to us, let us exercise them: if prophecy, in proportion to the faith; if ministry, ministering; if one is a teacher, in teaching; if one exhorts, in exhortation; if one contributes, in generosity; if one is over others, with diligence; if one does acts of mercy, with cheerfulness.
1Cor. 12:4	There are different kinds of spiritual gifts but the same Spirit.
1Cor. 12:28, 31	Some people God has designated in the church to be first, apostles; second, prophets; third, teachers; then, mighty deeds; then gifts of healing, assistance, administration, and various tongues. Strive eagerly for the greatest spiritual gifts.

1Cor. 13:2	And if I have the gift of prophecy and comprehend all mysteries and all knowledge; if I have all faith so as to move mountains but do not have love, I am nothing.
1Cor. 14:1	Pursue love, but strive eagerly for the spiritual gifts.
2Cor 9:15	Thanks be to God for this indescribable gift!
Eph. 2:8	For by grace you have been saved through faith, and this is not from you; it is the gift of God.
Eph. 3:7	Of this, I became a minister by the gift of God's grace that was granted me in accord with the exercise of his power.
Eph. 4:7	But grace was given to each of us according to the measure of Christ's gift.
1Tim. 4:14	Do not neglect the gift you have, which was conferred on you through the prophetic word with the imposition of hands.
2Tim. 1:6	For this reason, I remind you to stir into flame the gift of God that you have through the imposition of my hands.
Ja. 1:17	All good giving and every perfect gift is from above.
1Pet. 4:10	As each has received a gift, use it to serve one another as good stewards of God's varied grace.

GLORY

The glory of God
is a person
fully alive.

St. Irenaeus

GLORY

Glory means magnificence, splendor ... and for me glory has always been a little bit of a mystery. One day on retreat I asked God to teach me about glory. And God opened my eyes! Let me share my "Glory" story.

A friend of mine had moved to another town, about 30 miles away. She asked me to pick up her kids from her new apartment, and then bring them back to our town so they could go to school that day ... 6 am in the morning! Finding it hard to say no to such a special friend, I said, "Yes." But 6 am the next morning, I was wondering if I was crazy. Driving down the road I put in a music disc and a song came on about GLORY. Uplifting and energizing, the music awakened my spirit, and I was happy! Then the morning sunrise entered in while the song was playing. Morning light filtered through the blowing fields of amber grass until all seemed spun in gold. It was absolutely breathtaking! I even said, "How can it get better than this?" When, just as I was topping a hill, arose a huge, colorful hot air balloon. It looked as if it were rising from the road in front of me. I still can remember my forgetting to breathe for a moment, as I took it all in.

There is so much glory all around us if we but see. Like the beauty, in the beat of a hummingbird's wing, or the delicate blossoms on a cherry tree, that speak of the glory of God. One can feel the glory of God in the prayerful presence of people praying for someone's healing. Whenever a new born baby is placed in my arms, there is such an awesome presence of glory! It is times like this, that I find I cannot talk ... sacred silence enters in.

Where God is ... one will find glory; and since God is all around, so is glory. So the question arises: How can my life bring glory to God? For me, perhaps the moment I am facing the person who hurt me the most and somewhere find the love to forgive, I bring glory to God. I am still learning about this precious mystery ... glory.

Reflection Questions:

Recall key moments when you have experienced God's glory.

How might you become more aware of the glory of God in your life?

GLORY

Ex. 24:17-18   To the Israelites the glory of the LORD was seen as a consuming fire on the mountaintop. But Moses passed into the midst of the cloud as he went up on the mountain; and there he stayed for forty days and forty nights.

Ex. 29:43   There, at the altar, I will meet the Israelites: hence, it will be made sacred by my glory.

Tobit 12:6   Raphael called the two men aside privately and said to them: "Thank God! Give him the praise and the glory. Before all the living, acknowledge the many good things he has done for you, by blessing and extolling his name in song."

Job 29:20   My glory is fresh within me, / and my bow is renewed in my hand!

Ps. 3:4   But you, LORD, are a shield around me; /my glory, you keep my head high.

Ps. 8:5-6   What are humans that you are mindful of them, / mere mortals that you care for them?/ Yet you have made them little less than a god, /crowned them with glory and honor.

Ps.21:6-7   Great is his glory in your victory; / majesty and splendor you confer upon him./ You make him the pattern of blessings forever, / you gladden him with the joy of your presence.

Ps. 26:8   LORD, I love the house where you dwell, / the tenting-place of your glory.

Ps. 62:8   My safety and glory are with God, / my strong rock and refuge.

Ps. 63:2-3   O God, you are my God — / for you I long! / For you my body yearns; / for you my soul thirsts. / Like a land parched, lifeless, / and without water. / So I look to you in the sanctuary / to see your power and glory.

Ps. 71:8   My mouth shall be filled with your praise, / shall sing your glory every day.

Ps. 84:12   For a sun and a shield is the LORD God, / bestowing all grace and glory. / The LORD withholds no good thing / from those who walk without reproach.

Ps. 104:1   Bless the LORD, my soul! / LORD, my God, you are great indeed! / You are clothed with majesty and glory.

Ps. 105:3   Glory in his holy name; / rejoice, O hearts that seek the LORD!

Ps. 115:1   Not to us, LORD, not to us / but to your name give glory / because of your faithfulness and love.

Pro. 16:31   Gray hair is a crown of glory; / it is gained by virtuous living.

Pro. 19:11   It is good sense in a person to be slow to anger, / and it is his glory to overlook an offense.

Wis. 3:15   For the fruit of noble struggles is a glorious one; / and unfailing is the root of understanding.

Sir. 3:19   For great is the power of God; / by the humble he is glorified.

Sir. 17:23	No more can the dead give praise than those who have never lived; / they glorify the Lord who are alive and well.
Sir. 40:27	The fear of the Lord is a paradise of blessings; / its canopy, all that is glorious.
Sir. 45:26	And now bless the LORD / who has crowned you with glory! /May he grant you wisdom of heart.
Is. 6:3	"Holy, holy, holy is the LORD of hosts!" they cried one to the other. "All the earth is filled with his glory."
Is. 40:6	"All mankind is grass, / and all their glory like the flower of the field. / The grass withers, the flower wilts, / when the breath of the Lord blows upon it. / ... Though the grass withers and the flower wilts, / the word of our God stands forever."
Is. 43: 5, 7	Fear not, for I am with you; / from the east I will bring back your descendants, / from the west I will gather you. / ... Everyone who is named as mine, / whom I created for my glory, / whom I formed and made.
Is. 49:3	You are my servant, he said to me, / Israel, through whom I show my glory.
Is. 58:8	Then your light shall break forth like the dawn, / and your wound shall quickly be healed; / Your vindication shall go before you, / and the glory of the Lord shall be your rear guard.
Is. 60:1-2	Rise up in splendor! Your light has come, / the glory of the Lord shines upon you. / See, darkness covers the earth, / and thick clouds cover the peoples; / But upon you the Lord shines, / and over you appears his glory.

Is. 61:3   To place on those who mourn in Zion / a diadem instead of ashes, / To give them oil of gladness in place of mourning, / a glorious mantle instead of a listless spirit. / They will be called oaks of justice, / planted by the Lord to show his glory.

Is. 62:3   You shall be a glorious crown in the hand of the LORD, / a royal diadem held by your God.

Ez. 43:3-5   I fell prone as the glory of the LORD entered the temple by way of the gate which faces the east, but spirit lifted me up and brought me to the inner court. And I saw that the temple was filled with the glory of the Lord.

Zech. 2:9   But I will be for her an encircling wall of fire, says the LORD, and I will be the glory in her midst.

Mk. 13:26   And then they will see 'the Son of Man coming in the clouds' with great power and glory, and then he will send out the angels and gather [his] elect from the four winds, from the end of the earth to the end of the sky.

Lk. 2:14   Glory to God in the highest / and on earth peace to those on whom his favor rests.

Jn. 15:8   By this is my Father glorified, that you bear much fruit and become my disciples.

Jn. 17:22   And I have given them the glory you gave me, so that they may be one, as we are one.

Jn. 17:24   Father, they are your gift to me. I wish that where I am they also may be with me, that they may see my glory that you gave me, because you loved me.

Rom. 2:10   There will be glory, honor, and peace for everyone who does good.

Rom. 11:36   For from him and through him and for him are all things. To him be glory forever. Amen.

1Cor. 10:31   So whether you eat or drink, or whatever you do, do everything for the glory of God.

2Cor. 1:20   For however many are the promises of God, their Yes is in him; therefore, the Amen from us also goes through him to God for glory.

2Cor. 3:18   All of us, gazing with unveiled face on the glory of the Lord, are being transformed into the same image from glory to glory, as from the Lord who is the Spirit!

2Cor. 4:6   For God who said, "Let light shine out of darkness," has shone in our hearts to bring to light the knowledge of the glory of God on the face of [Jesus] Christ.

2Cor. 4:17   For this momentary light affliction is producing for us an eternal weight of glory beyond all comparison.

Eph. 1:18   May the eyes of [your] hearts be enlightened, that you may know what is the hope that belongs to his call what are the riches of glory in his inheritance among the holy ones.

Eph. 3:16   ...that he may grant you in accord with the riches of his glory to be strengthened with power through his spirit in the inner self.

Phil. 1:10-11 Discern what is of value, so that you may be pure and blameless for the day of Christ, filled with the fruit of righteousness that comes through Jesus Christ for the glory and praise of God.

Phil. 4:19 My God will fully supply whatever you need, in accord with his glorious riches in Christ Jesus.

Col. 3:4 When Christ your life appears, then you too will appear with him in glory.

1Thess. 2:19-20 For what is our hope or joy or crown to boast of in the presence of our Lord Jesus at his coming if not you yourselves? For you are our glory and joy!

2Thess 2:14 To this end he has [also] called you through our gospel to possess the glory of our Lord Jesus Christ.

1Pe. 1:6-7 In this you rejoice, although now for a little while you may have to suffer through various trials, so that the genuineness of your faith, more precious than gold that is perishable even though tested by fire, may prove to be for praise, glory, and honor at the revelation of Jesus Christ.

1Pe. 4:14 If you are insulted for the name of Christ, blessed are you, for the Spirit of glory and of God rests upon you.

1Pe. 5:10 The God of all grace who called you to his eternal glory through Christ [Jesus] will himself restore, confirm, strengthen, and establish you after you have suffered a little.

Rev. 21:23 The city had no need of sun or moon to shine on it, for the glory of God gave it light, and its lamp was the Lamb.

GOODNESS

God, of your goodness,
give me Yourself,
You are enough for me.

Julian of Norwich

GOODNESS

"God is good. All the time! All the time. God is good!" This is a favorite response in many retreat groups. I am reminded that goodness is a very special quality of God. Remembering the creation stories in Genesis, we see that everything that God created was good. So what does this say about us ... were we created in goodness?

Each little innocent baby is created by God; and what God creates is good! So what happened? What happened that so many of us, both young and old, have forgotten their goodness? How is it that we see the worst in ourselves and each other, rather than seeing the goodness? People could tell me 10 good things about myself. One person may say something they do not like about me. What do you think I remember? Yes, I remember the negative and put way too much emphasis on it. I'll play it over and over in my head. I will carry that as a burden, that I placed on myself. So how can I nurture goodness in myself?

When I think of goodness, a heart overflowing with love comes to mind. In the past, I believed that my goodness was because of my choices. Now I see that my goodness comes from the center of my being, where God dwells. Goodness comes from my cooperating with God's grace. If I am honest, that cooperation sometimes comes with much inner struggle. Letting goodness flow is not always easy. Goodness is a choice each of us must make.

An example of goodness for me is this very special Polish priest, Fr. Stan. Whatever he is doing ... praying, cooking, planting, or meetings, he brings the quality of simple goodness to all. His goodness reflects so beautifully the goodness of God. Father Stan's example of a good life encourages others to this virtue of goodness. In a world with so much negative news, I am encouraged by people like Father Stan. May my eyes be open to see the goodness in all ... may I choose to see the goodness in all!

Reflection Questions:

Who do you know that lives "goodness" out in everyday life?

How can you nurture goodness in yourself?

GOODNESS

Ps. 13:6	I trust in your faithfulness. / Grant my heart joy in your help, / That I may sing of the Lord, / "How good our God has been to me!"
Ps. 16:2	I say to the LORD, / you are my Lord, / you are my only good.
Ps. 21:4	For you welcomed him with goodly blessings; / you placed on his head a crown of pure gold.
Ps. 23:6	Only goodness and love will pursue me / all the days of my life; / I will dwell in the house of the Lord / all the days of my life.
Ps. 25:5	Guide me in your truth and teach me, / for you are God my savior. / For you I wait all the long day, / because of your goodness, Lord.
Ps. 25:8	Good and upright is the LORD, / who shows sinners the way.
Ps. 27:13	But I believe I shall enjoy the LORD's goodness / in the land of the living.
Ps. 31:20	How great is your goodness, LORD, / stored up for those who fear you.
Ps. 33:5	The LORD loves justice and right / and fills the earth with goodness.
Ps. 34:9	Learn to savor how good the LORD is; / happy are those who take refuge in him.

Ps. 34:15	Turn from evil and do good; / seek peace and pursue it.
Ps. 37:3	Trust in the LORD and do good / that you may dwell in the land and live secure.
Ps. 51:3	Have mercy on me, God, in your goodness; / in your abundant compassion blot out my offense.
Ps. 65:5	Happy the chosen ones you bring / to dwell in your courts. / May we be filled with the good things of your house.
Ps. 73:1	How good God is to the upright, / the Lord, to those who are clean of heart!
Ps. 73:28	As for me, to be near God is my good, / to make the Lord GOD my refuge.
Ps. 84:12	For a sun and shield is the LORD God, / bestowing all grace and glory. / The LORD withholds no good thing / from those who walk without reproach.
Ps. 100:5	Good indeed is the LORD, / Whose love endures forever, / whose faithfulness lasts through every age.
Ps. 103:5	Fills your days with good things; / your youth is renewed like the eagle's.
Ps. 107:9	For he satisfied the thirsty, / filled the hungry with good things.
Ps. 116:7	Return, my soul, to your rest; / the LORD has been good to you.
Ps. 116:12	How can I repay the LORD / for all the good done for me?

Ps. 133:1	How good it is, how pleasant, / where the people dwell as one!
Ps. 136:1	Praise the LORD, who is good; / God's love endures forever.
Ps. 145:9	The LORD is good to all, / compassionate to every creature.
Wis. 1:1	Love justice, you who judge the earth; / think of the LORD in goodness, / and seek him in integrity of heart.
Sir. 2:9	You who fear the LORD, hope for good things, / for lasting joy and mercy.
Sir. 12:1	If you do good, know for whom you are doing it, / and your kindness will have its effect.
Sir. 13:25	The sign of a good heart is a cheerful countenance.
Sir. 39:16	The works of God are all of them good; / in its own time every need is supplied.
Is. 63:7	The favors of the LORD I will recall, / the glorious deeds of the Lord, / Because of all he has done for us; / for he is good to the house of Israel.
Jer. 32:39	One heart and one way I will give them, that they may fear me always, to their own good and that of their children after them.
Jer. 33:9	Then Jerusalem shall be my joy, my praise, my glory, before all the nations of the earth, as they hear of all the good I will do among them.
Lam. 3:25	Good is the LORD to one who waits for him, / to the soul that seeks him.

Lam. 3:26	It is good to hope in silence / for the saving help of the LORD.
Lk. 6:45	A good person out of the store of goodness in his heart produces good.
Rom. 15:14	I myself am convinced about you, my brothers, that you yourselves are full of goodness, filled with all knowledge, and able to admonish one another.
Rom. 16:19-20	For while your obedience is known to all, so that I rejoice over you, I want you to be wise as to what is good, and simple as to what is evil; then the God of peace will quickly crush Satan under your feet.
2 Cor. 9:8	God is able to make every grace abundant for you, so that in all things, always having all you need, you may have an abundance for every good work.
Gal. 6:9	Let us not grow tired of doing good, for in due time we shall reap our harvest, if we do not give up.
Eph. 2:10	For we are his handiwork created in Christ Jesus for the good works that God has prepared in advance, that we should live in them.
Eph. 5:8-9	Live as children of light, for light produces every kind of goodness and righteousness and truth.
Col. 1:10	Live in a manner worthy of the Lord, so as to be fully pleasing, in every good work bearing fruit and growing in the knowledge of God.
Col. 2:5	For even if I am absent in the flesh, yet I am with you in spirit, rejoicing as I observe your goodness and the firmness of your faith in Christ.
1Th. 5:21	Test everything, retain what is good.

2Th. 1:11-12 We always pray for you, that our God may make you worthy of his calling and powerfully bring to fulfillment every good purpose and every effort of faith, that the name of our Lord Jesus may be glorified in you.

2Th. 2:16-17 May our Lord Jesus Christ himself and God our Father, who has loved us and given us everlasting encouragement and good hope through his grace, encourage your hearts and strengthen them in every good deed and word.

1Tim. 1:18-19 May you fight a good fight by having faith and a good conscience.

1Tim 4:4-5 For everything created by God is good, and nothing is to be rejected when received with thanksgiving, for it is made holy by the invocation of God in prayer.

1Tim. 6:18-19 Tell them to do good, to be rich in good works, to be generous, ready to share, thus accumulating as treasure a good foundation for the future, so as to win the life that is true life.

Titus 3:8 I want you to insist on these points, that those who have believed in God be careful to devote themselves to good works; these are excellent and beneficial to others.

Phm. 4-6 I give thanks to my God always, remembering you in my prayers, as I hear of the love and the faith you have in the Lord Jesus and for all the holy ones, so that your partnership in the faith may become effective in recognizing every good there is in us that leads to Christ.

Phm. 14   … but I did not want to do anything without your consent, so that the good you do might not be forced but voluntary.

Heb.13:16   Do not neglect to do good and to share what you have; God is pleased by sacrifices of that kind.

Ja. 3:13   Who among you is wise and understanding? Let him show his works by a good life in humility that comes from wisdom.

1Pe.2:15   For it is the will of God that by doing good you may silence the ignorance of foolish people.

1Pe. 4:19   Those who suffer in accord with God's will hand their souls over to a faithful creator as they do good.

3Jn. 11   Beloved, do not imitate evil but imitate good. Whoever does what is good is of God.

GRACE

Without the burden of afflictions
it is impossible to reach the height of grace.
The gift of grace increases
as the struggles increase.

St. Rose of Lima

GRACE

Grace, for me, was one of those elusive words, like a butterfly that you cannot seem to catch. However, when you are not looking for grace, it comes upon you! For me, it has been a lifelong search for an understanding of grace. Grace is not something I can define in the normal way but in my own creative way ...

Grace is like a soft gentle rain.
As it falls upon the earth,
it caresses your face
with such gentleness.
Like that rain,
grace nourishes and empowers us
with the very life and love of God!

I used to think of grace as a noun, something that could be gathered like a commodity. With wisdom finally sinking in, I see grace as a verb that is constantly active, moving, and transforming with the life and love of God!

As we all know the rains come in due time. We simply pray and wait with an openness of our spirit. We trust that the One who loves us, will "grace us" with that love when we need it. I don't know about you, but I am very "needy" on a daily basis. The problem is that I can be so busy, and so full of myself, that I am not always aware of my need for God's grace. With this lack of awareness, I forget to go to the One, who is the Giver of all Graces, and ASK! If we could see ... we would see God waiting with an abundance of grace, ready for us to simply open our hearts to receive!

May you open and receive all the grace
that God desires to give to you!

Reflection Questions:

Define grace in your own creative way.

How needy are you for God's grace?

GRACE

Ps. 33:18	The LORD's eyes are upon the reverent, / upon those who hope for his gracious help.
Ps. 67:2	May God be gracious to us and bless us; / may God's face shine upon us.
Ps. 70:2	Graciously rescue me, God! / Come quickly to help me, LORD!
Ps. 84:12	For a sun and shield is the LORD God, / bestowing all grace and glory.
Ps. 86:15	But you, Lord, are a merciful and gracious God, / slow to anger, most loving and true!
Ps.103:8	Merciful and gracious is the LORD, / slow to anger, abounding in kindness.
Ps. 116:5	Gracious is the LORD and just; / yes, our God is merciful.
Ps. 145:8	The LORD is gracious and merciful, / slow to anger and abounding in love.
Wis. 3:9	Those who trust in him shall understand truth, / and the faithful shall abide with him in love, / Because grace and mercy are with his holy ones.
Jn. 1:14	And the Word became flesh / and made his dwelling among us, / and we saw his glory, / the glory as of the Father's only Son, / full of grace and truth.

Jn. 1:16-17   From his fullness we have all received, grace in place of grace, because while the law was given through Moses, grace and truth came through Jesus Christ.

Acts 20:24   Yet I consider life of no importance to me, if only I may finish my course and the ministry that I received from the Lord Jesus, to bear witness to the gospel of God's grace.

Rom. 1:5   Through him we have received the grace of apostle-ship, to bring about the obedience of faith.

Rom. 3:24   They are justified freely by his grace through the redemption in Christ Jesus.

Rom. 5:20   The law entered in so that transgression might increase but, where sin increased, grace overflowed all the more.

Rom. 6:14   For sin is not to have any power over you, since you are not under the law, but under grace.

1Cor. 1:4   I give thanks to my God always on your account for the grace of God bestowed on you in Christ Jesus.

1Cor. 15:10   But by the grace of God I am what I am, and his grace to me has not been ineffective. Indeed, I have toiled harder than all of them; not I, however, but the grace of God [that is] with me.

2Cor. 4:15   Everything indeed is for you, so that the grace bestowed in abundance on more and more people may cause the thanksgiving to overflow for the glory of God.

2Cor. 9:8   God is able to make every grace abundant for you, so that in all things, always having all you need, you may have an abundance for every good work.

2Cor. 9:14	… while in prayer on your behalf they long for you, because of the surpassing grace of God upon you.
2Cor. 12:9	My grace is sufficient for you, for power is made perfect in weakness.
2Cor. 13:13	The grace of the Lord Jesus Christ and the love of God and the fellowship of the holy Spirit be with all of you.
Gal. 1:15	[God,] who from my mother's womb had set me apart and called me through his grace.
Eph. 1:5-6	… he destined us for adoption to himself through Jesus Christ, in accord with the favor of his will, for the praise of the glory of his grace that he granted us in the beloved.
Eph. 1:7	In him we have redemption by his blood, the forgiveness of transgressions, in accord with the riches of his grace that he has lavished upon us.
Eph. 2:4-5	But God, who is rich in mercy, because of the great love he had for us, even when we were dead in our transgressions, brought us to life with Christ (by grace you have been saved.)
Eph. 2:8	For by grace you have been saved through faith, and this is not from you; it is the gift of God.
Eph. 3:7	Of this I became a minister by the gift of God's grace that was granted me in accord with the exercise of his power.
Eph. 4:7	But grace was given to each of us according to the measure of Christ's gift.

Phil. 1:7   It is right that I should think this way about all of you, because I hold you in my heart, you who are all partners with me in grace, both in my imprisonment and in the defense and confirmation of the gospel.

Phil. 4:8   Finally, … whatever is true, whatever is honorable, whatever is just, whatever is pure, whatever is lovely, whatever is gracious, if there is any excellence and if there is anything worthy of praise, think about these things.

2Thess. 1:11-12   To this end, we always pray for you, that our God may make you worthy of his calling and powerfully bring to fulfillment every good purpose and every effort of faith, that the name of our Lord Jesus may be glorified in you, and you in him, in accord with the grace of our God and Lord Jesus Christ.

2Thess. 2:16-17   May our Lord Jesus Christ himself and God our Father, who has loved us and given us everlasting encouragement and good hope through his grace, encourage your hearts and strengthen them in every good deed and word.

1Tim. 1:14   Indeed, the grace of our Lord has been abundant, along with the faith and love that are in Christ Jesus.

2Tim. 1:9   He saved us and called us to a holy life, not according to our works but according to his own design and the grace bestowed on us in Christ Jesus before time began.

2Tim. 2:1   So you, my child, be strong in the grace that is in Christ Jesus.

Heb. 4:16   So let us confidently approach the throne of grace to receive mercy and to find grace for timely help.

Ja. 4:6	God resists the proud, / but gives grace to the humble.
1Pe. 1:13	Therefore, gird up the loins of your mind, live soberly, and set your hopes completely on the grace to be brought to you at the revelation of Jesus Christ.
1Pe. 2:19	For whenever anyone bears the pain of unjust suffering because of consciousness of God, that is a grace.
1Pe. 4:10	As each one has received a gift, use it to serve one another as good stewards of God's varied grace.
1Pe. 5:10	The God of all grace who called you to his eternal glory through Christ [Jesus] will himself restore, confirm, strengthen, and establish you after you have suffered a little.
2Pe. 1:2	May grace and peace be yours in abundance through knowledge of God and of Jesus our Lord.
2Pe. 3:18	But grow in grace and in the knowledge of our Lord and savior Jesus Christ.
2Jn. 1:3	Grace, mercy, and peace will be with us from God the Father and from Jesus Christ the Father's Son in truth and love.
Rev. 1:4	Grace to you and peace from him who is and who was and who is to come…

HEALING

Oh, how everything
that is suffered with love
is healed again!

St. Teresa of Avila

HEALING

As a child I thought that everything could come to healing with some Neosporin and a bandage. But then I grew older and discovered that the deepest hurts in need of healing were of the heart and mind. For years I struggled with how to find healing for these deep and dark places in myself. Healing was going to take time, precious time ... in God's time.

I had to come to a place where I was tired of carrying all the baggage of hurt and pain in my life. I set out on a journey of forgiveness so that I might release all the bitterness and anger from the past. If I truly believed that this healing is possible, then it would be! The secret for me was in the "key of forgiveness." I even had to forgive myself! It was only when I emptied myself of bitterness, unforgiveness, and lots of anger, that God could fill the void with the grace of healing love. Inner healing is a reality!

But Lord, what now? I look around and there are so many walking wounded. The earth is in need of healing. The seas and skies are polluted. Marriages and families are torn apart. Nation against nation are fighting for what? I want to bring healing to others, to the world. My inner need to "fix" everything keeps rising up. But I cannot "fix" people. I cannot simply pour the formula into them. I can only love them. And just maybe, my example of living with healing in my life, will encourage them to follow the path to Christ! Lord, we need your healing love!

Reflection Questions:

What do you need to be healed from?

What are you willing to release and forgive for that to happen?

How can you be a healing presence to others?

HEALING

Ex. 15:26   I, the LORD, am your healer!

Tobit 12:6-22   (Actually, the whole story is a great one of healing!)

Ps. 6:3   Have pity on me, LORD, for I am weak; / heal me, LORD, for my bones are trembling.

Ps. 30:3   O LORD, my God, / I cried out to you and you healed me!

Ps. 41:5   Once I prayed, "LORD, have mercy on me; / heal me, I have sinned against you."

Ps. 51:16   Rescue me from death, God, my saving God, / that my tongue may praise your healing power.

Ps. 103:2-4   Bless the LORD, my soul; / do not forget all the gifts of God, / Who pardons all your sins, / heals all your ills, / Delivers your life from the pit, / surrounds you with love and compassion.

Ps. 107:20   Sent forth the word to heal them, / snatched them from the grave.

Ps. 147:3   Heals the brokenhearted, / binds up their wounds.

Ecc. 3:3   … a time to heal …

Is. 19:22b   … he shall heal them: they shall turn to the LORD and he shall be won over and heal them.

Is. 53:5   But he was pierced for our offenses, / crushed for our sins, / Upon him was the chastisement that makes us whole, / by his stripes we were healed.

Is. 58:8	Then your light shall break forth like the dawn, / and your wounds shall quickly be healed.
Is. 61:1	The spirit of the Lord God is upon me, / because the Lord has anointed me; / He has sent me to bring glad tidings to the lowly; / to heal the brokenhearted, / To proclaim liberty the captives / and release to prisoners.
Jer. 3:22	Return, rebellious children, / and I will heal you of your rebelling. / "Here we are, we now come to you / because you are the Lord, our God."
Jer. 17:14	Heal me, Lord, that I may be healed; / save me, that I may be saved, / for it is you whom I praise.
Jer. 30:17	For I will restore you to health; / of your wounds I will heal you, says the Lord.
Jer. 33:6	Behold, I will treat and assuage the city's wounds; I will heal them, and reveal to them an abundance of lasting peace.
Hos. 14:5	I will heal their defection, / I will love them freely.
Mal. 3:20	But for you who fear my name, there will arise / the sun of justice with its healing rays.
Matt. 8:8	Lord, I am not worthy to have you enter under my roof; only say the word and my servant will be healed.
Lk. 6:19	Everyone in the crowd sought to touch him because power came forth from him and healed them all.

Lk. 8:47-48   Falling down before him, she explained in the presence of all the people why she had touched him and how she had been healed immediately. He said to her, "Daughter, your faith has saved you, go in peace."

1Cor. 12:4, 7, 9 There are different kinds of spiritual gifts but the same Spirit. To each individual the manifestation of the Spirit is given for some benefit ... to another gifts of healing by the one Spirit.

1Pe. 2:24   For by his wounds you have been healed.

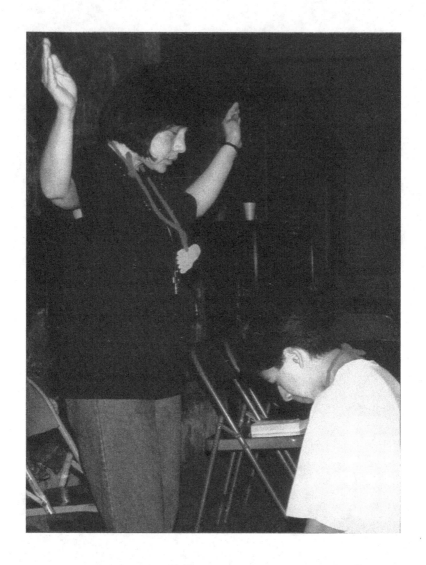

HEART

Don't lose heart. Carry on!
Carry on with that holy stubbornness
which in spiritual terms is
called perseverance.

St. Josemaria Escriva

HEART

Heart, what an image of love and of life! Spiritually, the word heart symbolizes the very center of our inner being ... the sacred place where Love dwells. To reflect on the word "heart" can lead us on a journey of self discovery and to God.

I lost my heart to two men ... the first was to Jesus and the second to my husband, Mike. I do not give my heart easily, but when I do, I give it fully. My heart has been well cared for through these two men! So the questions: How is my heart doing? Who is welcome in my heart? What restrictions do I place on who I will love and who I will not? What does my heart reveal about me?

The first time I reflected on these questions, many years ago, I discovered a lot about myself. I found myself more like Fort Knox! Having been hurt emotionally early in life, and carrying all that bitterness, I was in a protective mode. No one was getting in unless they were near perfect. Guess what? Most people in our lives are no where near perfect, therefore, I found myself very lonely. Perhaps that is why in discovering the gift of forgiveness, I finally found peace!

I like to take morning walks just before sunrise, when the day is still quiet. There is a song written by David Kauffman, a spirit-filled man, that calls forth my heart to surrender to God. And in the surrendering, asking God to ... Purify My Heart. Does my heart need purifying? Everyday! Being human, my heart is constantly being challenged to follow the false gods of this world. Everyday, I am encouraged by Ego to hold on to bitterness, anger and hurt. So what a great way to start my day, with this song in my heart, asking God to *purify my heart* once again. I am reminded that "conversion" is a daily process!

Whenever I am frightened, lonely, or hurting, I like to imagine God's heart. As God's child, I crawl close to the radiating warmth and the steady sound of His heartbeat. There I find I am welcomed, safe and loved! May you rediscover the wonders of God's heart on your faith journey! May you discover your own heart capable of great love as well!

Reflection Questions:

How is your heart doing these days?

What part of your heart have you surrendered to God?
What part are you holding back?

Have you imagined "your place" in God's heart?
Have you visited lately?

HEART

Deut. 6:5-6   Therefore, you shall love the LORD, your God, with all your heart, and with all your soul, and with all your strength. Take to heart these words which I enjoin on you today.

Deut. 30:6   The LORD, your God, will circumcise your hearts and the hearts of your descendants, that you may love the Lord, your God, with all your heart and all your soul, and so may live.

1Sam. 16:7   But the LORD said to Samuel: "Do not judge from his appearance or from his lofty stature, because I have rejected him. Not as man sees does God see, because man sees the appearance but the Lord looks into the heart."

1Ki. 3:9   Give your servant, therefore, an understanding heart to judge your people and to distinguish right from wrong.

1Ki. 8:58   May he draw our hearts to himself, that we may follow him in everything and keep the commands, statutes, and ordinances which he enjoined on our fathers.

1Chr. 22:19   Therefore, devote your hearts and souls to seeking the LORD your God.

1Chr. 28:9   As for you, Solomon, my son, know the God of your father and serve him with a perfect heart and a willing soul, for the Lord searches all hearts and understands all the mind's thoughts.

Ps. 13:6	I trust in your faithfulness, / Grant my heart joy in your help, / That I may sing of the Lord, "How good our God has been to me."
Ps. 15:1-2	LORD, who may abide in your tent? / Who may dwell on your holy mountain? / Whoever walks without blame, doing what is right, speaking truth from the heart.
Ps. 16:9	Therefore, my heart is glad, my soul rejoices; / my body also dwells secure.
Ps. 21:3	You have granted him his heart's desire; / you did not refuse the prayer of his lips.
Ps. 27:8	"Come," says my heart, "seek God's face;" / your face, LORD, do I seek.
Ps. 27:14	Wait for the LORD, take courage; / be stouthearted, wait for the Lord!
Ps. 28:7	The LORD is my strength and my shield, / in whom my heart trusted and found help. / So my heart rejoices; / with my song I praise my God.
Ps. 31:25	Be strong and take heart, / all you who hope in the LORD.
Ps. 37:4	Find your delight in the LORD / who will give you your heart's desire.
Ps. 51:12	A clean heart create for me, God; / renew in me a steadfast spirit.
Ps. 62:9	Trust God at all times, my people! / Pour out your hearts to God our refuge!
Ps. 73:26	God is the rock of my heart, my portion forever.

Ps. 84:6   Happy are those who find refuge in you, / whose hearts are set on pilgrim roads.

Ps. 86:11   Teach me, LORD, your way / that I may walk in your truth, / single-hearted and revering your name.

Ps. 86:12   I will praise you with all my heart, / glorify your name forever, Lord my God.

Ps. 105:3   Glory in his holy name; / rejoice, O hearts that seek the LORD!

Pro. 3:5-6   Trust in the LORD with all your heart, / on your own intelligence rely not; / In all your ways be mindful of him, / and he will make straight your paths.

Ecc. 5:19   For he will hardly dwell on the shortness of life, because God lets him busy himself with the joy of his heart.

So. 8:6   Set me as a seal on your heart, / as a seal on your arm.

Sir. 2:1-2   When you come to serve the LORD, / prepare yourself for trials. / Be sincere of heart and steadfast, / undisturbed in time of adversity.

Sir. 50:23   May he grant you joy of heart / and may peace abide among you!

Is. 35:4   Say to those whose hearts are frightened: / Be strong, fear not! / Here is your God, / he comes with vindication; / With divine recompense / he comes to save you.

Is. 60:5   Then you shall be radiant at what you see, / your heart shall throb and overflow, / For the riches of the sea shall be emptied out before you.

Jer. 15:16   When I found your words, I devoured them; / they became my joy and the happiness of my heart.

Jer. 20:9   I say to myself, I will not mention him, / I will speak in his name no more. / But then it becomes like fire burning in my heart, / imprisoned in my bones; / I grow weary holding it in, / I cannot endure it.

Jer. 24:7   I will give them a heart to understand that I am the LORD. They shall be my people and I will be their God.

Jer. 29:13-14   When you look for me, you will find me. Yes, when you seek me with all your heart, you will find me with you, says the Lord.

Jer. 31:33   I will place my law within them, and write it upon their hearts; I will be their God and they shall be my people.

Ez. 36:26   I will give you a new heart and place a new spirit within you, taking from your bodies your stony hearts and giving you natural hearts.

Joel 2:13   Rend your hearts, not your garments, / and return to the LORD, your God. / For gracious and merciful is he, / slow to anger, rich in kindness, / and relenting in punishment.

Matt. 5: 8   Blessed are the clean of heart, / for they shall see God.

Matt. 6:21   For where your treasure is, there also will your heart be.

Matt. 11:29   Take my yoke upon you and learn from me, for I am meek and humble of heart; and you will find rest for yourselves.

Mk. 11:23   Amen, I say to you, whoever says to this mountain, "Be lifted up and thrown into the sea," and does not doubt in his heart but believes that what he says will happen, it shall be done for him.

Mk. 12:30   You shall love the Lord your God with all your heart, with all your soul, with all your mind, and with all your strength.

Lk. 6:45   A good person out of the store of goodness in his heart produces good.

Lk. 8:15   But as for the seed that fell on rich soil, they are the ones who, when they heard the word, embrace it with a generous and good heart, and bear fruit through perseverance.

Lk. 10:27   You shall love the Lord, your God, with all your heart, with all your being, with all your strength, and with all your mind, and your neighbor as yourself.

Lk. 12:34   For where your treasure is, there also will your heart be.

Lk. 24:32   Were not our hearts burning [within us] while he spoke to us on the way and opened the scriptures to us?

Jn. 14:1   Do not let your hearts be troubled. You have faith in God; have faith also in me.

Jn. 16:22   But I will see you again, and your hearts will rejoice, and no one will take your joy away from you.

Rom. 10:8-9   "The word is near you, / in your mouth and in your heart." / ... For if you confess with your mouth that Jesus is Lord and believe in your heart that God raised him from the dead, you will be saved.

Eph. 1:18   May the eyes of [your] hearts be enlightened, that you may know what is the hope that belongs to his call, what are the riches of glory in his inheritance among the holy ones, and what is the surpassing greatness of his power for us who believe.

Eph. 3:17   … that Christ may dwell in your hearts through faith.

Phil. 2:1-2   If there is any encouragement in Christ, any solace in love, any participation in the Spirit, any compassion and mercy, complete my joy by being of the same mind, with the same love, united in heart, thinking one thing.

Phm. 20   Refresh my heart in Christ.

1Pe. 1:22   Since you have purified yourselves by obedience to the truth for sincere mutual love, love one another intensely from a [pure] heart.

2Pe. 1:19   Moreover, we possess the prophetic message that is altogether reliable. You will do well to be attentive to it, as to a lamp shining in a dark place, until day dawns and the morning star rises in your hearts.

HOLY

Our life is a journey
of growing in holiness,
day by day ...
letting God's love transform us
into the image of Jesus!

Patti King

HOLY

Holy ... consecrated, blessed, divine, sacred! It is easy to believe that God, Mary, and the saints are holy. We probably feel that sacred places like churches, shrines and special places are holy. But that's it. When we look at ourselves, we may draw the line, feeling that we are so unworthy and sinful and therefore we cannot be holy!

I have come to understand that holiness does not mean perfection (as humans see it); rather, holy means the presence of God. As in 1Peter 1:16, "Be holy because I [am] holy." Where God dwells is holy. So what does that say about you, if God dwells in you? After all, when you were baptized and received Confirmation, were you not anointed with oil? You were consecrated, blessed, set aside as God's own!

As I look back on my life, I can see how God, my special Spiritual Director, brought people into my life to help guide me on a path to holiness. Yes, I leave the path often and there is always someone who brings me back. This precious Divine Friend would take my worst possible life experiences and use them to teach me deeper truths about God and myself. Holiness comes from God's action in my life. God truly is good ... all the time!

But that brings on the problem, if I begin to see myself as holy, then what does that mean for my life? How I act? What I do? If we truly saw ourselves as God sees us, we probably would respond with love more, and not give in to those urges to act in an unacceptable way! Our words might be more uplifting than condemning. Our eyes might choose true things of beauty, rather than things that are smutty. Our ears might listen to music that uplifts the soul, rather than music that degrades humans. We just might stand up for another person, rather than join in on destroying them through idle gossip. I question myself more about what I say, or don't say; what I send in an email; how I take criticism, and how I forgive. Imagine, God tugging at your heart and saying:

"Just as I see you as holy, My child, look around …
holiness dwells all around you,
in all my children and creation.
Honor and respect all!"

Lord, help me to see how you make my life holy; and that of every person I meet.

Reflection Questions:

Bless yourself in some way to celebrate that holiness that dwells with you!

What needs to change in you that you might reflect that holiness more and more?

HOLY

Ex. 3:5	"Come, no nearer! Remove the sandals from your feet, for the place where you stand is holy ground."
Ex. 20:8	Remember to keep holy the sabbath day.
Lev. 11:44	For I, the LORD, am your God: and you shall make and keep yourselves holy, because I am holy.
Lev. 19:2	Be holy, for I, the LORD, your God, am holy.
Lev. 20:7	Sanctify yourselves, then, and be holy; for I, the LORD, your God, am holy.
Wis. 3:9	Those who trust in him shall understand truth, / and the faithful shall abide with him in love; / Because grace and mercy are with his holy ones, / and his care is with his elect.
Wis. 7:27-28	And passing into holy souls from age to age, / she produces friends of God and prophets. / For there is nought God loves, be it not one who dwells with Wisdom.
Is. 6:3	Holy, holy, holy is the LORD of hosts! … All the earth is filled with his glory!
Is. 35:8a, 9b	A highway will be there, / called the holy way. / It is for those with a journey to make, / and on it the redeemed will walk.

Is. 43:3-4	For I am the LORD, your God, / the Holy One of Israel, your savior. / I give Egypt as your ransom, / Ethiopia and Seba in return for you. / Because you are precious in my eyes / and glorious, and because I love you.
Is. 62:12	They shall be called the holy people, / the redeemed of the LORD, / And you shall be called "Frequented," / a city that is not forsaken.
Ez. 36:23b	Thus the nations shall know that I am the LORD, says the Lord GOD, when in their sight I prove my holiness through you.
Matt. 3:11	I am baptizing you with water, for repentance, but the one who is coming after me is mightier than I. I am not worthy to carry his sandals. He will baptize you with the holy Spirit and fire.
Matt. 28:19	Go, therefore, and make disciples of all nations, baptizing them in the name of the Father, and of the Son, and of the holy Spirit.
Jn. 20:22	And when he had said this, he breathed on them and said to them, "Receive the holy Spirit."
Acts 1:8	But you will receive power when the holy Spirit comes upon you, and you will be my witnesses ... to the ends of the earth.
Rom. 5:5	And hope does not disappoint, because the love of God has been poured out into our hearts through the holy Spirit that has been given to us.
Rom. 11:16	If the firstfruits are holy, so is the whole batch of dough; and if the root is holy, so are the branches.

Rom. 12:1   I urge you therefore, brothers, by the mercies of God, to offer your bodies as a living sacrifice, holy and pleasing to God, your spiritual worship.

Rom. 16:16   Greet one another with a holy kiss. All the churches of Christ greet you.

1Cor. 3:17   If anyone destroys God's temple, God will destroy that person; for the temple of God, which you are, is holy.

1Cor. 6:19-20   Do you not know that your body is a temple of the holy Spirit within you, whom you have from God, and that you are not your own? For you have been purchased at a price. Therefore, glorify God in your body.

2Cor. 7:1   Since we have these promises, beloved, let us cleanse ourselves from every defilement of flesh and spirit, making holiness perfect in the fear of God.

Eph. 1:4   He chose us in him, before the foundation of the world, to be holy and without blemish before him.

Eph. 1:18-19   May the eyes of [your] hearts be enlightened, that you may know what is the hope that belongs to his call, what are the riches of glory in his inheritance among the holy ones and what is the surpassing greatness of his power for us who believe.

Eph. 2:19   So then, you are no longer strangers and sojourners, but you are fellow citizens with the holy ones and members of the household of God.

Eph. 4:11-12   And he gave some as apostles, others as prophets, others as evangelists, others as pastors and teachers, to equip the holy ones for the work of ministry, for building up the body of Christ.

Eph. 4:24   Put on the new self, created in God's way in righteousness and holiness of truth.

Col. 1:3-4   We always give thanks to God, the Father of our Lord Jesus Christ, when we pray for you, for we have heard of your faith in Christ Jesus and the love that you have for all the holy ones.

Col. 3:12-13   Put on then, as God's chosen ones, holy and beloved, heartfelt compassion, kindness, humility, gentleness, and patience, bearing with one another and forgiving one another.

1Thes. 3:12-13   May the Lord make you increase and abound in love for one another and for all, just as we have for you, so as to strengthen your hearts, to be blameless in holiness before our God and Father at the coming of our Lord Jesus with all his holy ones.

1Thes. 5:23   May the God of peace himself make you perfectly holy and may you entirely, spirit, soul, and body, be preserved blameless for the coming of our Lord Jesus Christ.

1Tim. 4:4-5   For everything created by God is good, and nothing is to be rejected when received with thanksgiving, for it is made holy by the invocation of God in prayer.

2Tim. 1:9   He saved us and called us to a holy life, not according to our works but according to his own design and the grace bestowed on us in Christ Jesus before time began.

Heb. 3:1   Therefore, holy "brothers," sharing in a heavenly calling, reflect on Jesus, the apostle and high priest of our confession.

Heb. 12:14	Strive for peace with everyone, and for that holiness without which no one will see the Lord.
1Pe. 1:15-16	He who called you is holy, be holy yourselves in every aspect of your conduct, for it is written, "Be holy because I [am] holy."
1Pe. 2:4-5	Come to him, a living stone, rejected by human beings but chosen and precious in the sight of God, and like living stones, let yourselves be built into a spiritual house to be a holy priesthood to offer spiritual sacrifices acceptable to God through Jesus Christ.
1Pe. 2:9	But you are "a chosen race, a royal priesthood, a holy nation, a people of his own, so that you may announce the praises" of him who called you out of darkness into his wonderful light.
1Jn. 2:20	You have the anointing that comes from the holy one, and you all have knowledge.
Jude 20	But you, beloved, build yourselves up in your most holy faith; pray in the holy Spirit.

HOPE

The future belongs
to those who give the
next generation
reason to hope.

Pierre Teilhard De Chardin

Hope

Starlight, star bright, first star I see tonight
I wish I may, I wish I might
have the wish I wish tonight!

Hope … to wish for, anticipate, desire. As children, we often would wait to see who would spot the first star. With childlike wonder, we would make that hopeful wish. I don't know about you, but I still get excited when I see that first star. However, the things I hope for are so much more important than when I was little.

Interesting, when I think of hope, I think of times of darkness waiting for that beacon of light. One dark night hope took on a deeper meaning for me as a teenager. Sitting high in a tree praying for a glimmer of hope, I received a heart message from God:

"Hold on, it won't be like this forever. There
is a future of hope for you."

The stars seemed to twinkle a little brighter, and calm came over me. I held on to that beacon of hope! I trusted that God saw the bigger picture and that it would be good. And it was!

We cannot truly understand hope unless we are at the end of our rope and there is no where else to turn. Then, hope becomes a beacon, a lifeline to hang onto. We grow closer to God, who is our ultimate Hope, especially:

at the bedside of a very sick loved one …
in the doctor's office waiting to hear the results of a medical test …
a parent waiting for their teenager in the wee hours of the morning …
someone in a deep depression or addiction at the end of their rope.

Hope is our companion on this journey of life. Without hope life is dark. Therefore, we all grasp for some hope that "all will be well." Hope seems to keep us looking forward, like waiting for the dawn to bring morning's light! At a time in history when things can look very dark, God needs us all to be "bringers of hope!" We are challenged to keep our lanterns lit and to take hope into our homes, our communities, and our world! One of the greatest gifts we can give to those who sit in darkness and shame is glimmers of hope!

Reflection Questions:

What do you hope for?

How can you be a beacon of hope for others?

HOPE

Job 11:18 You shall be secure, because there is hope; / you shall look around you and lie down in safety.

Job 14:7-9 For a tree there is hope, / if it be cut down, that it will sprout again / and that its tender shoots will not cease. / Even though its root grow old in the earth, / and its stump die in the dust, / Yet at the first whiff of water it may flourish again / and put forth branches like a young plant.

Ps. 31:25 Be strong and take heart, / all you who hope in the LORD.

Ps. 33:18 But the LORD's eyes are upon the reverent, / upon those who hope for his gracious help.

Ps. 33:22 May your kindness, LORD, be upon us; / we have put our hope in you.

Ps. 39:8 Lord, what future do I have? / You are my only hope.

Ps. 62:6 My soul, be at rest in God alone, / from whom comes my hope.

Ps.71:5 You are my hope, Lord; / my trust, God, from my youth.

Ps. 71:6 On you I depend since birth; / from my mother's womb you are my strength; / my hope in you never wavers.

Ps. 119:49 Remember your word to your servant / by which you give me hope.

Ps. 119:81   My soul longs for your salvation; / I put my hope in your word.

Ps. 119:114   You are my refuge and shield; / in your word I hope.

Ps. 119:147   I rise before dawn and cry out; / I put my hope in your words.

Ps. 131:3   Israel, hope in the LORD, / now and forever.

Ps. 146:5   Happy those whose help is Jacob's God, / whose hope is in the LORD, their God.

Pro. 10:28   The hope of the just brings them joy.

Sir. 2:6   Trust God and he will help you; / make straight your ways and hope in him.

Sir. 34:13   Lively is the courage of those who fear the LORD, / for they put their hope in their savior.

Sir. 34:14   He who fears the LORD is never alarmed, / never afraid; for the LORD is his hope.

Is. 40:31   They that hope in the LORD will renew their strength, / they will soar as with eagles' wings; / They will run and not grow weary; / they will walk and not grow faint.

Jer. 17:7   Blessed is the man who trusts in the LORD, / whose hope is the LORD.

Jer. 29:11   For I know well the plans I have in mind for you, says the LORD, plans for your welfare not for woe! plans to give you a future full of hope.

Lam. 3:26   It is good to hope in silence / for the saving help of the LORD.

Acts 2:26   Therefore my heart has been glad and my tongue has exulted; / my flesh too will dwell in hope.

Rom. 5:3-5   We even boast of our afflictions, knowing that affliction produces endurance, and endurance, proven character, and proven character, hope, and hope does not disappoint, because the love of God has been poured out into our hearts through the holy Spirit that has been given to us.

Rom. 8:25   But if we hope for what we do not see, we wait with endurance.

Rom. 12:12   Rejoice in hope, endure in affliction, persevere in prayer.

Rom. 15:13   May the God of hope fill you with all joy and peace in believing, so that you may abound in hope by the power of the holy Spirit.

1Cor. 13:7   [Love] It bears all things, believes all things, hopes all things, endures all things.

Gal. 5:5   For through the Spirit, by faith, we await the hope of righteousness.

Eph. 1:18   May the eyes of [your] hearts be enlightened, that you may know what is the hope that belongs to his call, what are the riches of glory in his inheritance among the holy ones.

Eph. 4:4   One body and one Spirit, as you were also called to the one hope of your call.

Phil. 1:20   My eager expectation and hope is that I shall not be put to shame in any way, but that with all boldness, now as always, Christ will be magnified in my body, whether by life or by death.

Phil. 3:12   It is not that I have already taken hold of it or have already attained perfect maturity, but I continue my pursuit in hope that I may possess it, since I have indeed been taken possession of by Christ [Jesus].

Col. 1:3-5   We always give thanks to God, the Father of our Lord Jesus Christ, when we pray for you, for we have heard of your faith in Christ Jesus and the love that you have for all the holy ones because of the hope reserved for you in heaven.

Col. 1:22-23   He has now reconciled in his fleshly body through his death, to present you holy, without blemish, and irreproachable before him, provided that you persevere in the faith, firmly grounded, stable, and not shifting from the hope of the gospel that you heard.

Col. 1:26-27   But now it has been manifested to his holy ones, to whom God chose to make known the riches of the glory of this mystery among the Gentiles; it is Christ in you, the hope for glory.

1Th. 1:2-3   We give thanks to God always for all of you, re-membering you in our prayers, unceasingly calling to mind your work of faith and labor of love and endurance in hope of our Lord Jesus Christ.

1Th. 2:19-20   For what is our hope or joy or crown to boast of in the presence of our Lord Jesus at his coming if not you yourselves? For you are our glory and joy.

1Th. 5:8   But since we are of the day, let us be sober, putting on the breastplate of faith and love and the helmet that is hope of salvation.

2Th. 2:16-17   May our Lord Jesus Christ himself and God our Father, who has loved us and given us everlasting encouragement and good hope through his grace, encourage your hearts and strengthen them in every good deed and word.

1Tim. 4:10   For this we toil and struggle, because we have set our hope on the living God, who is the savior of all, especially of those who believe.

Heb. 10:23   Let us hold unwaveringly to our confession that gives us hope, for he who made the promise is trustworthy.

1Pe. 1:3   Blessed be the God and Father of our Lord Jesus Christ, who in his great mercy gave us a new birth to a living hope through the resurrection of Jesus Christ.

1Pe. 1:13   Therefore, gird up the loins of your mind, live soberly, and set your hopes completely on the grace to be brought to you at the revelation of Jesus Christ.

1Pe. 3:15-16   Always be ready to give an explanation to anyone who asks you for a reason for your hope, but do it with gentleness and reverence, keeping your conscience clear.

1Jo. 3:3   Everyone who has this hope based on him makes himself pure, as he is pure.

HUMILITY

To arrive at being all
desire to be nothing ...
in this nakedness
the spirit finds its rest,
for when it covets nothing,
nothing raises it up,
and nothing weighs it down,
because it is in the
center of its humility.

John of the Cross

HUMILITY

Humility is a word that most of us struggle with, in that we often perceive this word to be one of weakness. Humility comes from the Latin word humus, meaning of the earth. I have come to explain humility, or being humble, this way:

> To be humble means to know yourself
> ~ no more or no less ~
> than who you simply are in God's eyes.

We are encouraged in scripture not to exalt ourselves. However, do we realize that to be less than who we were created to be, devalues the creation that God made. A mistake that many of us make in our daily lives!

Marianne Williamson from <u>A Return to Love</u> challenges us:

> Who are you to be less than who you were created to be.
> "Our deepest fear is not that we are inadequate. Our deepest fear is that we are powerful beyond measure. It is our light, not our darkness that most frightens us. We ask ourselves, Who am I to be brilliant, gorgeous, talented, fabulous? Actually, who are you *not* to be? You are a child of God. Your playing small does not serve the world. There is nothing enlightened about shrinking so that other people won't feel insecure around you. We are all meant to shine, as children do. We were born to make manifest the glory of God that is within us. It's not just in some of us; it's in everyone. And as we let our own light shine, we unconsciously give other people permission to do the same. As we are liberated from our own fear, our presence automatically liberates others."

When we are in the presence of someone truly humble, they radiate peace, joy, freedom, and truth! There is nothing in them that has to protect the EGO, no barriers to defend themselves … they are just simply present! May we choose to grow in true humility, that we may be truly free!

Reflection Questions:

Who do you know who is truly humble?

What needs to change in you that you may live a humble life?

Humility

2Chr. 7:14   And if my people, upon whom my name has been pronounced, humble themselves and pray, and seek my presence and turn from their evil ways, I will hear them from heaven and pardon their sins and revive their land.

Ps. 25:9   [The Lord] guides the humble rightly, / and teaches the humble the way.

Ps. 51:19   My sacrifice, God, is a broken spirit; / God, do not spurn a broken, humbled heart.

Pro. 11:2   When pride comes, disgrace comes; / but with the humble is wisdom.

Pro. 15:33   The fear of the LORD is training for wisdom, / and humility goes before honors.

Pro. 16:19   It is better to be humble with the meek / than to share plunder with the proud.

Pro. 29:23   Man's pride causes his humiliation, / but he who is humble of spirit obtains honor.

Sir. 1:24   For fear of the LORD is wisdom and culture; / loyal humility is his delight.

Sir. 2:17   Those who fear the LORD prepare their hearts / and humble themselves before him.

Sir. 3:17   My son, conduct your affairs with humility, / and you will be loved more than a giver of gifts.

Sir. 3:18   Humble yourself the more, the greater you are, / and you will find favor with God.

Sir. 3:19	For great is the power of God; / by the humble he is glorified.
Sir. 10:27	My son, with humility have self-esteem; / prize yourself as you deserve.
Dan. 10:12	Fear not, Daniel, … from the first day you made up your mind to acquire understanding and humble yourself before God, your prayer was heard.
Mic. 6:8	You have been told, O man, what is good, / and what the LORD requires of you: / Only to do right and to love goodness, / and to walk humbly with your God.
Zeph. 2:3	Seek the LORD, all you humble of the earth, / who have observed his law; / Seek justice, seek humility; / perhaps one day you may be sheltered / on the day of the Lord's anger.
Zeph. 3:12	But I will leave as a remnant in your midst / a people humble and lowly, / Who shall take refuge in the name of the Lord.
Matt. 11:29	Take my yoke upon you and learn from me, for I am meek and humble of heart; and you will find rest for yourselves.
Matt. 18:4	Whoever humbles himself like this child is the greatest in the kingdom of heaven.
Lk. 14:11	For everyone who exalts himself will be humbled, but the one who humbles himself will be exalted.
Acts 20:19	I served the Lord with all humility and with the tears and trials that came to me.
Eph. 4:1-2	I … urge you to live in a manner worthy of the call you have received, with all humility and gentleness, with patience, bearing with one another through love.

Phil. 2:3	Do nothing out of selfishness or out of vainglory; rather, humbly regard others as more important than yourselves.
Phil. 2:8	… he humbled himself, / becoming obedient to death, / even death on a cross.
Phil. 4:12	I know indeed how to live in humble circumstances; I know also how to live with abundance.
Col. 3:12	Put on then, as God's chosen ones, holy and beloved, heartfelt compassion, kindness, humility, gentleness, and patience.
Ja. 1:21	Humbly welcome the word that has been planted in you and is able to save your souls.
Ja. 3:13	Who among you is wise and understanding? Let him show his works by a good life in the humility that comes from wisdom.
Ja. 4:6-7	But he bestows a greater grace; therefore, it says: / "God resists the proud, / but gives grace to the humble" / So submit yourselves to God.
Ja. 4:10	Humble yourselves before the Lord and he will exalt you.
1Pe. 3:8	Finally, all of you, be of one mind, sympathetic, loving toward one another, compassionate, humble.
1Pe. 5:5	All of you, clothe yourselves with humility in your dealings with one another.
1Pe. 5:6	So humble yourselves under the mighty hand of God, that he may exalt you in due time.

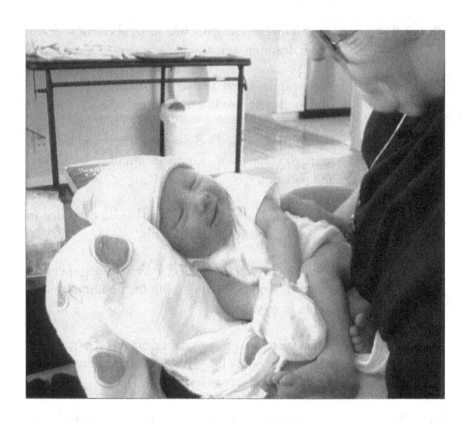

JOY

The fullness of joy
is to behold
God in everything!

Julian of Norwich

JOY

JOY is a word that cannot be contained by simply using letters, rather envision:

colorful balloons,
kids playing in the water sprinkler
and
joy that just bubbles up and explodes into giggles!

However, joy is so much deeper than fun and laughter. Joy is a gift of God that comes from deep within the very center of our being. Even in the difficult times of our life, we can find the "strength of joy" to see us through. What a delight for the one who lives with true joy in everyday life ... no matter what!

As we look at the cross, we are reminded of the great sacrifice of Jesus, yet the cross is also a symbol of Christian joy. A mother giving birth goes through great agony; yet beneath her pain is expectant joy! I remember going to visit a special friend who was dying of cancer. In spite of the heaviness of her life, knowing she was leaving teenage children and her worry for them, there was true joy! She kept singing a song about those "streets of gold" in heaven. I was at her side when she took her last breath ... such radiant joy.

At bible study we would gather and someone would say, "Did you hear about _____? He/she died yesterday." While the rest of us would get very sad, there was one who saw this event very differently. A precious older woman, Marion, would just light up, from the bottom of her toes right up to those brightly lit eyes and say, "Praise the Lord, another one has gone home." She said that she always knew when another precious person was going home, because this one rosebush would put off a single rose ... even in winter! Her infectious belief in life after death would have us all aglow with joy! This was our Marion; loveable, joyful and so faith-filled!

Marion, was not afraid of anything, she just trusted the Lord. She truly lived what she had professed, even when she discovered that she was dying. Really, she planned her own party before she died, so that she could enjoy everyone. She sent out invitations, supplied refreshments and lots of laughter! You could have written the word JOY on this woman's face. There was no fear, she was beaming with faith! Little did she know that I was watching her closely, for she was teaching me about living a life of true JOY!

Reflection Questions:

How can you cultivate a spirit of joy in your life?
Are you a joy-bringer to others?
What will you do this day to celebrate joy!

JOY

Ne. 8:10 Do not be saddened this day, for rejoicing in the LORD must be your strength!

Ps. 13:6 I trust in your faithfulness. / Grant my heart joy in your help, / That I may sing of the Lord. / "How good our God has been to me!"

Ps. 21:7 You make him the pattern of blessings forever, / you gladden him with the joy of your presence.

Ps. 28:7 The LORD is my strength and my shield, / in whom my heart trusted and found help. / So my heart rejoices; / with my song I praise my God.

Ps. 34:6 Look to God that you may be radiant with joy / and your faces may not blush for shame.

Ps. 47:2 All you peoples, clap your hands; / shout to God with joyful cries.

Ps. 51:14 Restore my joy in your salvation; / sustain in me a willing spirit.

Ps. 63:7-8 When I think of you upon my bed, / through the night watches I will recall / That you indeed are my help, / and in the shadow of your wings I shout for joy.

Ps. 89:16-17 Happy the people who know you, LORD, / who walk in the radiance of your face. / In your name they sing joyfully all the day; / at your victory they raise the festal shout.

Ps. 90:14	Fill us at daybreak with your love, / that all our days we may sing for joy.
Ps. 94:18-19	When I say, "My foot is slipping," / your love, LORD, holds me up. / When cares increase within me, / your comfort gives me joy.
Ps. 100:1-2	Shout joyfully to the LORD, all you lands; / worship the LORD with cries of gladness; / come before him with joyful song.
Ps. 105:3	Glory in his holy name; / rejoice, O hearts that seek the LORD!
Ps. 118:24	This is the day the LORD has made; / let us rejoice in it and be glad.
Ps. 126:5	Those who sow in tears / will reap with cries of joy.
Ps. 149:5	Let the faithful rejoice in their glory, / cry out for joy at their banquet.
Pro. 17:22	A joyful heart is the health of the body.
Ecc. 5:19	For he will hardly dwell on the shortness of his life, because God lets him busy himself with the joy of his heart.
Sir. 1:10	Fear of the LORD warms the heart, / giving gladness and joy and length of days.
Sir. 2:9	You who fear the LORD, hope for good things, / for lasting joy and mercy.
Sir. 26:2	A worthy wife brings joy to her husband, / peaceful and full is his life.

Sir. 30:16 — No treasure greater than a healthy body; / no happiness, than a joyful heart!

Sir. 50:23 — May he grant you joy of heart / and may peace abide among you.

Is. 12:3 — With joy you will draw water / at the fountain of salvation, and say on that day: / Give thanks to the Lord, acclaim his name; / among the nations make known his deeds.

Is. 35:1-2 — The desert and the parched land will exult; / the steppe will rejoice and bloom. / They will bloom with abundant flowers, / and rejoice with joyful song.

Is. 35:10 — Those whom the LORD has ransomed will return / and enter Zion singing, / crowned with everlasting joy; / They will meet with joy and gladness, / sorrow and mourning will flee.

Is. 51:3 — Joy and gladness shall be found in her, / thanksgiving and the sound of song.

Is. 55:12 — Yes, in joy you shall depart, / in peace you shall be brought back; / Mountains and hills shall break out in song before you, /and all the trees of the countryside shall clap their hands.

Is. 61:10 — I rejoice heartily in the LORD, / in my God is the joy of my soul.

Is. 65:18 — There shall always be rejoicing and happiness / in what I create; / For I create Jerusalem to be a joy / and its people to be a delight.

Jer. 15:16 — When I found your words, I devoured them; / they became my joy and the happiness of my heart.

Jer. 31:13 I will turn their mourning into joy, / I will console and gladden them after their sorrows.

Jer. 33:9 Then Jerusalem shall be my joy, my praise, my glory, before all the nations of the earth, as they hear of all the good I will do among them.

Zeph. 3:14 Shout for joy, O daughter Zion! / sing joyfully, O Israel! / Be glad and exult with all your heart!

Zeph. 3:17 The LORD, your God, is in your midst, / a mighty savior; / He will rejoice over you with gladness, / and renew you in his love, / He will sing joyfully because of you.

Matt. 13:44 The kingdom of heaven is like a treasure buried in a field, which a person finds and hides again, and out of joy goes and sells all that he has and buys the field.

Matt. 25:21 His master said to him, "Well done, my good and faithful servant. Since you were faithful in small matters, I will give you great responsibilities. Come, share your master's joy."

Lk. 1:46-47 My soul proclaims the greatness of the Lord; / my spirit rejoices in God my savior.

Lk. 2:10 Do not be afraid; for behold, I proclaim to you good news of great joy that will be for all the people.

Lk. 6:23 Rejoice and leap for joy on that day! Behold, your reward will be great in heaven. For their ancestors treated the prophets in the same way.

Lk. 15:7 I tell you, in just the same way there will be more joy in heaven over one sinner who repents than over ninety-nine righteous people who have no need of repentance.

Lk. 15:9-10	And when she does find it, she calls together her friends and neighbors and says to them, "Rejoice with me because I have found the coin that I lost." In just the same way, I tell you, there will be rejoicing among the angels of God over one sinner who repents.
Lk. 15:32	But now we must celebrate and rejoice, because your brother was dead and has come to life again; he was lost and has been found.
Jn. 15:11	I have told you this so that my joy might be in you and your joy might be complete.
Jn. 16:20	Amen, amen, I say to you, you will weep and mourn, while the world rejoices; you will grieve, but your grief will become joy.
Jn. 16:22	So you also are now in anguish. But I will see you again, and your hearts will rejoice, and no one will take your joy away from you.
Jn. 16:24	Until now you have not asked anything in my name: ask and you will receive, so that your joy may be complete.
Rom. 14:17	For the kingdom of God is not a matter of food and drink, but of righteousness, peace and joy in the holy Spirit.
Rom. 15:13	May the God of hope fill you with all joy and peace in believing, so that you may abound in hope by the power of our holy Spirit.
2Cor. 7:4	I have great confidence in you, I have great pride in you; I am filled with encouragement, I am overflowing with joy all the more because of all our affliction.

Gal. 5:22-23   In contrast, the fruit of the Spirit is love, joy, peace, patience, kindness, generosity, faithfulness, gentleness, self-control.

Phil. 1:3-4   I give thanks to my God at every remembrance of you, praying always with joy in my every prayer.

Phil. 2:2   … complete my joy by being of the same mind, with the same love, united in heart, thinking one thing.

Phil. 4:1   Therefore, my brothers, whom I love and long for, my joy and crown, in this way stand firm in the Lord, beloved.

Phil. 4:4   Rejoice in the Lord always, I shall say it again: rejoice!

1Th. 2:19-20   For what is our hope or joy or crown to boast of in the presence of our Lord Jesus at his coming if not you yourselves? For you are our glory and joy.

Ja. 1:2-3   Consider it all for joy, my brothers, when you encounter various trials, for you know that the testing of your faith produces perseverance.

1Pe. 1:8   Although you have not seen him you love him; even though you do not see him now yet believe in him, you rejoice with an indescribable and glorious joy.

3Jn. 4   Nothing gives me greater joy than to hear that my children are walking in the truth.

LIGHT

People are like stained-glass windows.
They sparkle and shine when the sun is out,
but when the darkness sets in
their true beauty is revealed
only if there is light from within.

Elisabeth Kubler-Ross

LIGHT

And let there be light! We flip a switch and we have light. How easy we have it in our warm comfortable homes. Bright sunlight, soft moonlight or a glowing candle, provides guidance and comfort. During an outage we come to a standstill. Trying to find matches for a candle, we run into walls and stub our toes. If light is so important to our lives, then how much more important is spiritual light, the light of Christ!

Jesus came and said,

" I am the Light of the World"
Jn. 8:12

and that light, made all the difference! It is this sacred light that guides my heart and soul in the way I should go. The light of Christ, flows into the recesses of my deepest self and shows me the hidden shadow areas that need healing and tending. For many of us, this could be threatening. We spend a lot of energy guarding our heart, so we don't have to see what is there. Sometimes we need courage to let the "Light of Christ" show us our true selves. This light warms my heart when the world seems so dark and uncaring. Like sunlight to a flower, this light nurtures my spiritual growth.

We are also told in the gospel of Matthew,

"You are the light of the world."
Matt. 5:14

We are to be a light to others who are in darkness, lighting the world with Christ's love and good news. I wonder how often we have missed the mark when we should have been a light for someone else. Perhaps we just didn't want to be bothered. Maybe it is time to take those bushel baskets off our light and just shine!

Patti King

One of my favorite stories is called, <u>A Trail Of Light</u>.

> Nineteenth-century writer and social reformer John Ruskin
> stood watching a lamplighter who went, torch in hand, from
> one post to another. As the man went down the street, his
> receding figure became dimmer and dimmer, but he left
> behind him a line of lights brightly burning. Ruskin then
> exclaimed, "There, that is what I mean by a real Christian!
> You can trace his course by the lights that he leaves burning.
> It is our job to keep the lights burning!"

Reflection Questions:

If you were to describe yourself as a light, what kind of light would you
be? & Why?

Where in your life does God need to shed some light right now?

LIGHT

Gen. 1:3-4	Then God said, "Let there be light," and there was light. God saw how good the light was.
Job 28:11	He probes the wellsprings of the streams, / and brings hidden things to light.
Job 29:3	While he kept his lamp shining above my head, / and by his light I walked through darkness.
Job 38:19	Which is the way to the dwelling place of light?
Ps. 4:7	LORD, show us the light of your face!
Ps. 18:29	You, LORD, give light to my lamp; / my God brightens the darkness about me.
Ps. 25:6-7	Remember your compassion and love, O LORD; / for they are ages old. / Remember no more the sins of my youth; / remember me only in light of your love.
Ps. 27:1	The LORD is my light and my salvation; /whom do I fear?
Ps. 43:3	Send your light and fidelity, / that they may be my guide.
Ps. 97:11	Light dawns for the just; / gladness, for the honest of heart.
Ps. 119:105	Your word is a lamp for my feet, / a light for my path.
Ps. 119:130	The revelation of your words sheds light, / gives understanding to the simple.

Ps. 139:11-12	If I say, "Surely darkness shall hide me, / and night shall be my light"— / Darkness is not dark for you, / and night shines as the day. / Darkness and light are but one.
Sir. 11:21	Trust in the LORD and wait for his light.
Sir. 26:16-17	Like the sun rising in the LORD's heavens, / the beauty of a virtuous wife is the radiance of her home. / Like the light which shines above the holy lampstand, / are her beauty of face and graceful figure.
Is. 9:1	The people who walked in darkness / have seen a great light; / Upon those who dwell in the land of gloom / a light has shone.
Is. 42:6	I, the LORD, have called you for the victory of justice, / I have grasped you by the hand; / I formed you, and set you / as a covenant of the people, / a light for the nations.
Is. 49:6	It is too little, he says, for you to be my servant, / to raise up the tribes of Jacob, / and restore the survivors of Israel; / I will make you a light to the nations, / that my salvation may reach to the ends of the earth.
Is. 58:8	Then your light shall break forth like the dawn, / and your wound shall quickly be healed.
Is. 58:10	If you bestow your bread on the hungry / and satisfy the afflicted; / Then light shall rise for you in the darkness, / and the gloom shall become for you like midday.
Is. 60:1	Rise up in splendor! Your light has come, / the glory of the Lord shines upon you.
Is. 60:19	No longer shall the sun / be your light by day, / Nor the brightness of the moon / shine upon you at night;

/ The Lord shall be your light forever, / your God shall be your glory.

Is. 60:20 No longer shall your sun go down, / or your moon withdraw, / For the LORD will be your light forever, / and the days of your mourning shall be at an end.

Dan. 2:22 He reveals deep and hidden things / and knows what is in the darkness, / for the light dwells with him.

Matt. 4:16 … the people who sit in darkness / have seen a great light, / on those dwelling in a land overshadowed by death / light has arisen.

Matt. 5:14 You are the light of the world. A city set on a mountain cannot be hidden.

Matt. 5:15 Nor do they light a lamp and then put it under a bushel basket; it is set on a lampstand, where it gives light to all in the house.

Matt. 5:16 Just so, your light must shine before others, that they may see your good deeds and glorify your heavenly Father.

Matt. 10:27 What I say to you in the darkness, speak in the light.

Matt. 11:30 For my yoke is easy, and my burden light.

Matt. 17:2 And he was transfigured before them; his face shone like the sun and his clothes became white as light.

Lk. 12:35-36 Gird your loins and light your lamps and be like servants who await their master's return.

Jn. 1:4 … through him was life, / and this life was the light of the human race.

Jn. 1:5	The light shines in the darkness, / and the darkness has not overcome it.
Jn. 3:21	Whoever lives the truth comes to the light, so that his works may be clearly seen as done in God.
Jn. 8:12	Jesus spoke to them again, saying, "I am the light of the world. Whoever follows me will not walk in darkness, but will have that light of life."
Jn. 12:35	Jesus said to them, "The light will be among you only a little while. Walk while you have the light, so that darkness may not overcome you."
Jn. 12:36	"While you have the light, believe in the light, so that you may become children of the light."
Jn. 12:46	"I came into the world as light, so that everyone who believes in me might not remain in darkness.
Acts 13:47	For so the Lord has commanded us, "I have made you a light to the Gentiles, that you may be an instrument of salvation to the ends of the earth."
Rom. 13:12	… the night is advanced, the day is at hand. Let us then throw off the works of darkness [and] put on the armor of light.
2Cor. 4:6	For God who said, "Let light shine out of darkness," has shone in our hearts to bring to light the knowledge of the glory of God on the face of [Jesus] Christ.
2Cor. 4:17	For this momentary light affliction is producing for us an eternal weight of glory beyond all comparison.
Eph. 5:8	For you were once darkness, but now you are light in the Lord. Live as children of light.

Eph. 5:9	For light produces every kind of goodness and righteousness and truth.
Eph. 5:13-14a	… but everything exposed by the light becomes visible, for everything that becomes visible is light.
Eph.5:14b	"Awake, O sleeper, / and arise from the dead, / and Christ will give you light!"
Phil. 2:14-15	Do everything without grumbling or questioning, that you may be blameless and innocent, children of God without blemish in the midst of a crooked and perverse generation, among whom you shine like lights in the world.
1Pe. 2:9	But you are "a chosen race, a royal priesthood, a holy nation, a people of his own, so that you may announce the praises" of him who called you out of darkness into his wonderful light.
1Jn. 1:5	God is light, and in him there is no darkness at all.
1Jn. 1:7	But if we walk in the light as he is in the light, then we have fellowship with one another, and the blood of his Son Jesus cleanses us from sin.
1Jn. 2:9-10	Whoever says he is in the light, yet hates his brother, is still in the darkness. Whoever loves his brother remains in the light, and there is nothing in him to cause a fall.
Rev. 21:23-24	The city had no need of sun or moon to shine on it, for the glory of God gave it light, and its lamp was the Lamb. The nations will walk by its light.
Rev. 22:5	Night will be no more, nor will they need light from lamp or sun, for the Lord God shall give them light, and they shall reign forever and ever.

LISTEN

Each day at the Center is punctuated
by the bells of St. Gerard's Church calling to us,
"Listen" they seem to say, "remember what you are all about!"
Listen to the bells ring in the deepest part of your heart,
calling to you, "Come, aside and rest with me awhile."

Deborah Hanus

LISTEN

One of the most loving actions we can do for another is to …

LISTEN: Have an attitude of attentiveness,
letting nothing distract us!
Being totally present to the other.

That is hard, for we are so easily distracted. Often we will listen with one ear, while looking to our own interest, or trying to do other things at the same time. There was a time in our culture when we had supper as a family. One table, the same time every night and we listened to each other during the meal. In our busy world that is happening so seldom. But our need to be listened to is great, and when we find that person who truly listens to us … that is love!

With our ears we can listen to what is being said; with our eyes we can listen even deeper by observing the way a person sits, uses their hands and especially to watch their eyes. But we can also listen with our hearts, picking up even deeper meanings. Good listening is an art! We spend our whole lives learning to listen.

How well do we listen to God? Do we listen attentively to the scripture readings in church or do we daydream until it is over? When we pray, who does all the talking, or does God get a chance? Being silent doesn't come easy, especially for me. I try; but the distractions in my life often feel like a three ring circus. Just try to be quiet and attentive to listen to God and the noises fill your head and heart. Images become a parade of problems, things to do, people to call. To simply breath, being conscious of deep slow breaths will help quiet the mind, body and spirit.

Once in great sadness in prayer, I was babbling everything in my heart, with tears flowing down my cheeks. A very sacred moment came upon me. I truly felt a finger touch my lips and say, "Hush. Let me simply love you!" Wrapped in great love, the One Who Loves me, calmed my very being.

Practice the art of listening, especially in prayer and you may discover God saying to your heart:

> "Let me love you. Let me fill you with what you need.
> Let Me be enough for you."

Reflection Questions:

How can I become a better listener? with others? with God?

Take a walk or sit outside and truly listen to creation. Journal what you experience.

LISTEN

1Sam. 3:10	Speak, for your servant is listening.
1Ki. 10:8	Happy are your men, happy these servants of yours, who stand before you always and listen to your wisdom.
2Chr. 6:19	Look kindly on the prayer and petition of your servant, O LORD, my God, and listen to the cry of supplication your servant makes before you.
2Chr. 6:21	Listen from your heavenly dwelling, and when you have heard, pardon.
2Chr. 20:20	Listen to me! ... Trust in the LORD, your God, and you will be found firm. Trust in his prophets and you will succeed.
Ps. 10:17	You listen, LORD, to the needs of the poor; / you encourage them and hear their prayers.
Ps. 45:11	Listen, my daughter, and understand; / pay me careful heed.
Ps. 55:2-3	Listen, God, to my prayer; / do not hide from my pleading; / hear me and give answer.
Ps. 61:2	Hear my cry, O God, / listen to my prayer!
Ps. 71:2	In your justice rescue and deliver me; / listen to me and save me!
Ps. 78:1	Attend, my people, to my teaching; / listen to the words of my mouth.

Ps. 81:14-15	But even now if my people would listen, / if Israel would walk in my paths, / In a moment I would subdue their foes.
Ps. 85:9	I will listen for the word of God; / surely the LORD will proclaim peace / To his people, to the faithful, / to those who trust in him.
Ps. 86:6	LORD, hear my prayer; / listen to my cry for help.
Ps. 116:1	I love the LORD, who listened / to my voice in supplication.
Ps. 140:7	I say to the LORD; You are my God: / listen, LORD, to the words of my prayer.
Ps. 141:1	LORD, I call to you; / come quickly to help me; / listen to my plea when I call.
Ps. 143:1	LORD, hear my prayer; / in your faithfulness listen to my pleading; / answer me in your justice.
Pro. 19:20	Listen to counsel and receive instruction, / that you may eventually become wise.
So. 8:13	O garden-dweller, / my friends are listening for your voice, / let me hear it!
Sir. 6:33	If you are willing to listen, you will learn; / if you give heed, you will be wise.
Sir. 33:4	Prepare your words and you will be listened to; / draw upon your training, and then give your answer.
Sir 39:13	Listen, my faithful children: open up your petals, / like roses planted near running waters.
Is. 48:12	Listen to me, Jacob, / Israel, whom I named!

Is. 49:1-3   Hear me, O coastlands, / listen, O distant peoples. / The LORD called me from birth, / from my mother's womb he gave me my name. / He made of me a sharp-edged sword / and concealed me in the shadow of his arm. / He made me a polished arrow, / in his quiver he hid me. / You are my servant, he said to me, / Israel, through whom I show my glory.

Is. 51:1   Listen to me, you who pursue justice, / who seek the LORD; / Look to the rock from which you were hewn, / to the pit from which you were quarried.

Is. 55:3   Come to me heedfully, / listen, that you may have life. / I will renew with you the everlasting covenant.

Jer. 7:23   Listen to my voice; then I will be your God, and you shall be my people. Walk in all the ways that I command you, so that you may prosper.

Jer. 11:4   Listen to my voice and do all that I command you. Then you shall be my people, and I will be your God.

Jer. 29:12   When you call me, when you go to pray to me, I will listen to you.

Matt. 17:5   While he was still speaking, a bright cloud cast a shadow over them, then from the cloud came a voice that said, "This is my beloved Son, with whom I am well pleased; listen to him."

Matt. 18:15-17   If your brother sins [against you,] go and tell him his fault between you and him alone. If he listens to you, you have won over your brother. If he does not listen, take one or two others along with you, so that 'every fact may be established on the testimony of two or three witnesses.' If he refuses to listen to them, tell the church. If he refuses to listen even to the church, then treat him as you would a Gentile or a tax collector.

Mk. 6:11   Whatever place does not welcome you or listen to you, leave there and shake the dust off your feet in testimony against them.

Lk. 21:38   And all the people would get up early each morning to listen to him in the temple area.

Acts 26:3   Therefore I beg you to listen patiently.

LOVE

A blessed thing it is
for any man or woman to have a friend,
one human soul whom we can trust utterly,
who knows the best and worst of us,
and who loves us in spite of all our faults.

Charles Kingsley

LOVE

Love is a word with many depths, yet in English love covers everything. But in Greek we have 3 ways to view the word love; my personal version!

Eros: I love chocolate cake; or whatever pleases me.
Filial: Brotherly love; friendship.
Agape: faithful, unconditional; I would die for you love!

The question for me is:
How do I love? With conditions?
With an attitude, what's in it for me?
Or can I love truly seeking the best for the other?
Can I allow the other to be who they are, without trying to change them, or judge them? Where can I learn how to love more perfectly?

In Jer.31:3 we hear these beautiful words …

With age-old love I have loved you.

WOW! God has loved me before I came to be, before I proved my worth, before I even knew that I was loved! So many times, when we step out in faith and love, we find ourselves hurt and in pain. So the next time love comes calling, we do not give our hearts … just a toe. And so it is with God, because people judge us harshly and reject us when they see our faults, we may think God will do so as well. How do we learn to love? Usually there is someone who loves us unconditionally. This may be a family member, a teacher, someone at church or a friend. For me, it was through the love of my husband. Never had I experienced such unconditional love. One day I realized that, my husband's love was just a reflection of the great love God has for me. That is what we can do for each other … love as God loves us; or at least to be a reflection of that great love!

If all people knew that they were loved, I believe great healing would take place. Marriages would flourish, nations would live in peace … if only! So remember always:

YOU ARE LOVED!

Reflection Questions:

When is the last time you simply sat and "let God love you"?

How can God perfect your love?

What needs to change in you for this to happen?

LOVE

Deut. 30:19-20 Choose life, then, that you and your descendants may live, by loving the LORD, your God, heeding his voice, and holding fast to him.

Ps. 18:2 I love you, LORD, my strength.

Ps. 23:6 Only goodness and love will pursue me / all the days of my life; / I will dwell in the house of the Lord / for years to come.

Ps. 25:6 Remember your compassion and love, O LORD; / for they are ages old.

Ps. 25:7 Remember no more the sins of my youth; / remember me only in light of your love.

Ps. 26:3 Your love is before my eyes; / I walk guided by your faithfulness.

Ps. 31:22 Blessed be the LORD, / who has shown me wondrous love.

Ps. 32:10 Love surrounds those who trust in the LORD.

Ps. 36:8 How precious is your love, O God! / We take refuge in the shadow of your wings.

Ps. 45:8 You love justice and hate wrongdoing; / therefore God, your God, has anointed you!

Ps. 69:17 Answer me, LORD, in your generous love; / in your great mercy turn to me.

Ps. 85:11	Love and truth will meet; / justice and peace will kiss.
Ps. 86:5	Lord, you are kind and forgiving, / most loving to all who call on you.
Ps. 90:14	Fill us at daybreak with your love, / that all our days we may sing for joy.
Ps. 94:18	When I say, "My foot is slipping," / your love, LORD, holds me up.
Ps. 106:1	Give thanks to the LORD, who is good, / whose love endures forever.
Ps. 145:8	The LORD is gracious and merciful, / slow to anger and abounding in love.
Pro. 7:18	"Come let us drink our fill of love, / until morning, let us feast on love."
Pro. 10:12	Hatred stirs up disputes, / but love covers all offenses.
So. 1:4	With you we rejoice and exult, / we extol your love; it is beyond wine; / how rightly you are loved!
So. 1:4	You are loved!
So. 2:4	He brings me into the banquet hall / and his emblem over me is love.
So. 2:10	My lover speaks; he says to me, / "Arise, my beloved, my beautiful one, / and come!"
So. 7:7	How beautiful you are, how pleasing, / my love, my delight

So. 8:6	Set me as a seal on your heart, / as a seal on your arm; / For stern as death is love.
So. 8:7	Deep waters cannot quench love, / nor floods sweep it away. / Were one to offer all he owns to purchase love, / he would be roundly mocked.
Wis. 7:27-28	And passing into holy souls from age to age, / she produces friends of God and prophets. / For there is nought God loves, be it not one who dwells with Wisdom.
Sir. 34:16	The eyes of the LORD are upon those who love him; / he is their mighty shield and strong support.
Is. 43:4	Because you are precious in my eyes / and glorious, and because I love you.
Jer. 31:3	With age-old love I have loved you; / so I have kept my mercy toward you.
Mic. 6:8	You have been told, O man, what is good, / and what the LORD requires of you: / Only to do right and to love goodness, / and to walk humbly with your God.
Zep. 3:17	He will rejoice over you with gladness, / and renew you in his love.
Matt. 5:44	But I say to you, love your enemies, and pray for those who persecute you.
Lk. 10:27	You shall love the Lord, your God, with all your heart, with all your being, with all your strength, and with all your mind, and your neighbor as yourself.
Jn. 3:16	For God so loved the world that he gave his only Son, so that everyone who believes in him might not perish but might have eternal life.

Jn. 12:25	Whoever loves his life loses it, and whoever hates his life in this world will preserve it for eternal life.
Jn. 13:34	I give you a new commandment: love one another. As I have loved you, so you also should love one another.
Jn. 13:35	This is how all will know that you are my disciples, if you have love for one another.
Jn. 14:21	Whoever has my commandments and observes them is the one who loves me. And whoever loves me will be loved by my Father, and I will love him and reveal myself to him.
Jn. 14:23	Jesus answered and said to him, "Whoever loves me will keep my word, and my Father will love him, and we will come to him and make our dwelling with him."
Jn. 15:9	As the Father loves me, so I also love you. Remain in my love.
Jn. 15:12	This is my commandment: love one another as I have loved you.
Jn. 15:13	No one has greater love than this, to lay down one's life for one's friends.
Jn. 17:26	I made known to them your name and I will make it known, that the love with which you loved me may be in them and I in them.
Rom. 5: 5	...and hope does not disappoint, because the love of God has been poured out into our hearts through the holy Spirit that has been given to us.
Rom. 8:28	We know that all things work for good for those who love God, who are called according to his purpose.

Rom. 8:38-39	For I am convinced that neither death, nor life, nor angels, nor principalities, nor present things, nor future things, nor powers, nor height, nor depth, nor any other creature will be able to separate us from the love of God in Christ Jesus our Lord.
Rom. 12:9	Let love be sincere; hate what is evil, hold on to what is good.
1Cor. 13:4	Love is patient, love is kind.
1Cor. 13:7-8	[Love] bears all things, believes all things, hopes all things, endures all things. Love never fails.
1Cor. 13:13	So faith, hope, love remain, these three; but the greatest of these is love.
1Cor. 16:14	Your every act should be done with love.
Gal. 2:20	Yet I live, no longer I, but Christ lives in me; insofar as I now live in the flesh, I live by faith in the Son of God who has loved me.
Gal. 5:22-23	In contrast, the fruit of the Spirit is love, joy, peace, patience, kindness, generosity, faithfulness, gentleness, self-control.
Eph. 3:17-19	…. and that Christ may dwell in your hearts through faith; that you, rooted and grounded in love, may have strength to comprehend with all the holy ones what is the breadth and length and height and depth, and to know the love of Christ that surpasses knowledge, so that you may be filled with all the fullness of God.
Eph. 4: 1-2 I	… urge you to live in a manner worthy of the call you have received, with all humility and gentleness, with patience, bearing with one another through love.

Eph. 4: 15   Living the truth in love, we should grow in every way into him who is the head, Christ.

Phil. 2:1-2   If there is any encouragement in Christ, any solace in love, any participation in the Spirit, any compassion and mercy, complete my joy by being of the same mind, with the same love, united in heart, thinking one thing.

Col. 3:14   And over all these put on love, that is, the bond of perfection.

1Th. 1:2-4   We give thanks to God always for all of you, remembering you in our prayers, unceasingly calling to mind your work of faith and labor of love and endurance in hope of our Lord Jesus Christ, before our God and Father, knowing, brothers loved by God, how you were chosen.

1Th. 5:8   But since we are of the day, let us be sober, putting on the breastplate of faith and love and the helmet that is hope for salvation.

2Th. 1:3   We ought to thank God always for you, brothers, as it is fitting, because your faith flourishes ever more, and the love of every one of you for one another grows ever greater.

2 Th. 3:5   May the Lord direct your hearts to the love of God and to the endurance of Christ.

2Tim. 1:7   For God did not give us a spirit of cowardice but rather of power and love and self-control.

1Pet. 1:22   Since you have purified yourselves by obedience to the truth for sincere mutual love, love one another intensely from a [pure] heart.

1Pet. 4:8	Above all, let your love for one another be intense, because love covers a multitude of sins.
1Jn. 3:18	Children, let us love not in word or speech but in deed and truth.
1Jn. 4:11-12	Beloved, if God so loved us, we also must love one another. No one has seen God. Yet, if we love one another, God remains in us, and his love is brought to perfection in us.
1Jn. 4:16	God is love, and whoever remains in love remains in God and God in him.
1Jn. 4:18	There is no fear in love, but perfect love drives out fear because fear has to do with punishment, and so one who fears is not yet perfect in love.

MERCY

May the greatest of all divine attributes,
that of unfathomable mercy,
pass through my heart and soul
to my neighbor.

St. Maria Faustina Kowalkska

MERCY

For many years I believed that mercy meant … pity or sympathy. Therefore, to me mercy was a negative word, one I didn't want. Mercy really took on a special significance when I heard of Sister Faustina's vision of the Divine Mercy. This vision of a loving heart pouring forth mercy changed my way of seeing this precious word. Jesus' eyes and hands in the picture speak of compassion, forgiveness, kindness, and generosity! It is as if Jesus invites you and me to open up our hearts and receive! Oh, to simply stand under those healing rays and just let mercy flow over and through me!

There is a song by Michael John Poirier, <u>Ocean of Mercy</u>, that so beautifully brings to mind, heart and soul, the meaning of mercy.

"Fly into the ocean of my mercy,
come and find perfect peace.
Fly into the ocean of my mercy,
open up to receive …"

Michael imagines God's mercy as an ocean. I see an ocean as vast, active, transforming … and so is God's mercy! Can you imagine jumping freely into this "ocean of mercy?" God is not miserly and stingy with love and mercy; but generous beyond telling! All we have to do is open and receive this great gift.

What an image to ponder … an ocean of mercy! Anyone want to take a dip?

Reflection Questions:

How do you describe the word mercy?

How have you experienced the Lord's great mercy?

Patti King

How do you in return, extend mercy to others?
    ... closed tightly ...
    ... a drippy faucet ...
    ... carefully released flow ...
    ... open the floodgates ...

MERCY

Ex. 15:13   In your mercy you led the people you redeemed; / in your strength you guided them to your holy dwelling.

2Chr. 30:9   For merciful and compassionate is the LORD your God, and he will not turn away his face from you if you return to him.

Tobit 3:2   You are righteous, O Lord, / and all your deeds are just; / All your ways are mercy and truth; / you are the judge of the world.

Tobit 8:16   Blessed are you, who have made me glad; / what I feared did not happen. / Rather you have dealt with us / according to your great mercy.

Ps. 27:7   Hear my voice, LORD, when I call; / have mercy on me and answer me.

Ps. 51:3   Have mercy on me, God, in your goodness; / in your abundant compassion blot out my offense.

Ps. 57:2   Have mercy on me, God, / have mercy on me. / In you I seek shelter. / In the shadow of your wings I seek shelter / till harm pass by.

Ps. 69:17   Answer me, LORD, in your generous love, / in your great mercy turn to me.

Ps 103:8   Merciful and gracious is the LORD, / slow to anger, abounding in kindness.

Ps. 109:21   But you, LORD, my God, / deal kindly with me for your name's sake; / in your great mercy rescue me.

Ps. 112:1, 4	Happy are those who fear the LORD, / who greatly delight in God's commands. / They shine through the darkness, a light for the upright; / they are gracious, merciful, and just.
Ps. 116:5	Gracious is the LORD and just; / yes, our God is merciful.
Ps. 119:58	I entreat you with all my heart; / have mercy on me in accord with your promise.
Ps. 130:1-2	Out of the depths I call to you, LORD; / Lord, hear my cry! / May your ears be attentive / to my cry for mercy.
Wis. 3:9	Those who trust in him shall understand truth, / and the faithful shall abide with him in love: / Because grace and mercy are with his holy ones.
Wis. 15:1	But you, our God, are good and true, / slow to anger, and governing all with mercy.
Sir. 2:7	You who fear the LORD, wait for his mercy.
Sir. 2:9	You who fear the LORD, hope for good things, / for lasting joy and mercy.
Sir. 2:11	Compassionate and merciful is the LORD; / he forgives sins, he saves in time of trouble.
Sir. 17:24	How great the mercy of the LORD, / his forgiveness of those who return to him!
Sir. 51:8	I remembered the mercies of the LORD, / his kindness through ages past; / For he saves those who take refuge in him, / and rescues them from every evil.
Sir. 51:29	Let your spirits rejoice in the mercy of God.

Is. 54:10	Though the mountains leave their place / and the hills be shaken, / My love shall never leave you / nor my covenant of peace be shaken, / says the Lord, who has mercy on you.
Jer. 31:3	With age-old love I have loved you; / so I have kept my mercy toward you.
Hos. 2:21	I will espouse you to me forever; / I will espouse you in right and in justice, / in love and in mercy.
Joel 2:13	Rend your hearts, not your garments, / and return to the LORD, your God. / For gracious and merciful is he, / slow to anger, rich in kindness, / and relenting in punishment.
Matt. 5:7	Blessed are the merciful, / for they will be shown mercy.
Matt. 9:13	Go and learn the meaning of the words, 'I desire mercy, not sacrifice,' I did not come to call the righteous but sinners.
Lk. 1:49-50	The Mighty One has done great things for me, / and holy is his name. / His mercy is from age to age / to those who fear him.
Lk. 1:77-78	… to give his people knowledge of salvation / through the forgiveness of their sins, / because of the tender mercy of our God / by which the daybreak from on high will visit us …
Lk. 6:36	Be merciful, just as [also] your Father is merciful.
Lk. 10:37	"The one who treated him with mercy." Jesus said to him, "Go and do likewise."
Lk. 18:13	"O God, be merciful to me a sinner."

Rom. 9:15   For he says to Moses, / "I will show mercy to whom I will, / I will take pity on whom I will."

Rom. 9:23-24   This was to make known the riches of his glory to the vessels of mercy, which he has prepared previously for glory, namely, us whom he has called.

Eph. 2:4-5   But God, who is rich in mercy, because of the great love he had for us, even when we were dead in our transgressions, brought us to life with Christ.

Phil. 2:1-2   If there is any encouragement in Christ, any solace in love, any participation in the Spirit, any compassion and mercy, complete my joy by being of the same mind, with the same love, united in heart, thinking one thing.

Tit. 3:4-5   But when the kindness and generous love / of God our savior appeared, / not because of any righteous deeds we had done / but because of his mercy, / he saved us through the bath of rebirth / and renewal by the holy Spirit.

Heb. 4:16   So let us confidently approach the throne of grace to receive mercy and to find grace for timely help.

Ja. 3:17   But the wisdom from above is first of all pure, then peaceable, gentle, compliant, full of mercy and good fruits, without inconstancy or insincerity.

1Pe. 1:3   Blessed be the God and Father of our Lord Jesus Christ, who in his great mercy gave us a new birth to a living hope through the resurrection of Jesus Christ from the dead.

1Pe. 2:9-10 You are "a chosen race, a royal priesthood, a holy nation, a people of his own, so that you may announce the praises" of him who called you out of darkness into his wonderful light. / Once you were "no people" / but now you are God's people; / you "had not received mercy" / but now you have received mercy.

Jude 1-2 To those who are called, beloved in God the Father and kept safe for Jesus Christ: may mercy, peace, and love be yours in abundance.

Jude 21 Keep yourselves in the love of God and wait for the mercy of our Lord Jesus Christ that leads to eternal life.

OPEN

Open my eyes to the beauty
that surrounds me
that I may walk through this day
with the kind of awareness
that calls forth grateful living.

Macrina Wiederkehr

OPEN

Open ... now that sounds like an easy enough word, or is it? We would all like to think that we are open. But are we? Prejudice fills our heart where we didn't expect it. Individualism permeates our being, and says, "I can do what I want." No matter how hard we try, we find ourselves still sinful, committing the same sin we confessed before! Is it any wonder that we close ourselves up to protect ourselves?

If we are truly honest with ourselves, we might ask the questions:

> What resistance do I have to being open to God?
> Is it fear that God might see me as I truly am?
> What if God asks more of me than I want to give?
> Will God encourage me to change?
> Perhaps, God will want me to forgive "this person,"
> and I want to hang on to this bitterness longer!

As long as I stay closed up in my spirit, the warming rays of God's love and light cannot reach me. Graces, like soft falling rain cannot penetrate my defenses.

I love the image from Sirach 39:13 ...

> Open up your petals,
> like roses planted near running waters.

It is this image I take to prayer and imagine my soul opening to the warm rays of God's love ... trusting in God's tender care! To open for me means to be vulnerable and so in the opening ... I need to trust!

> Thank you, God, the Master Gardener,
> for continually encouraging me
> to open to You. You never give up!

Reflection Questions:

How open are you to God?
    Wide open …
    Open, but can shut very quickly …
    Half way open …
    You need a crowbar …
What resistance do you find in yourself to being open to God? & Why?

OPEN

Deut. 15:11 The needy will never be lacking in the land; that is why I command you to open your hand to your poor and needy kinsman in your country.

Deut. 28:12 The LORD will open up for you his rich treasure house of the heavens, to give your land rain in due season, blessing all your undertakings, so that you will lend to many nations and borrow from none.

2Ki. 19:16 Incline your ear, O LORD, and listen! Open your eyes, O LORD, and see!

2Chr. 6:40 My God, may your eyes be open and your ears attentive to the prayer of this place.

Ps. 40:7 Sacrifice and offering you do not want; / but ears open to obedience you gave me.

Ps. 51:17 Lord, open my lips; / my mouth will proclaim your praise.

Ps. 78:2 I will open my mouth in story, / drawing lessons from of old.

Ps. 81:11 I, the LORD, am your God, / who brought you up from the land of Egypt. / Open wide your mouth that I may fill it.

Ps. 119:18 Open my eyes to see clearly / the wonders of your teachings.

Ps. 119:131 I sigh with open mouth, / yearning for your commands.

Ps. 145:16 You open wide your hand / and satisfy the desire of every living thing.

Pro. 8:6 Give heed! for noble things I speak; / honesty opens my lips.

Pro. 31:8-9 Open your mouth in behalf of the dumb, / and for the rights of the destitute; / Open your mouth, decree what is just, / defend the needy and the poor!

Sir. 39:6 His care is to seek the LORD, his Maker, / to petition the Most High, / To open his lips in prayer, / to ask pardon for his sins. / Then, if it pleases the Lord Almighty, / he will be filled with the spirit of understanding: / He will pour forth his words of wisdom / and in prayer give thanks to the Lord.

Sir. 39:13 Listen, my faithful children; open up your petals, / like roses planted near running waters.

Is. 35:4-5 Say to those whose hearts are frightened: / Be strong, fear not! / Here is your God, / he comes with vindication; / With divine recompense / he comes to save you. / Then will the eyes of the blind be opened.

Is. 42:6-7 I, the LORD, have called you for the victory of justice, / I have grasped you by the hand; / I formed you, and set you / as a covenant of the people, / a light for the nations, / To open the eyes of the blind, / to bring out prisoners from confinement, / and from the dungeon, those who live in darkness.

Is. 45:1 Thus says the LORD to his anointed, Cyrus, / whose right hand I grasp, / Subduing nations before him, / and making kings run in his service, / Opening doors before him / and leaving the gates unbarred.

Is. 45:8   Let justice descend, O heavens, like dew from above, / like gentle rain let the skies drop it down. / Let the earth open and salvation bud forth; / let justice also spring up!

Is. 50:4   The Lord GOD has given me / a well-trained tongue, / That I might know how to speak to the weary / a word that will rouse them. / Morning after morning / he opens my ear that I may hear.

Is. 53:7   Though he was harshly treated, he submitted / and opened not his mouth; / Like a lamb led to the slaughter / or a sheep before the shearers, / he was silent and opened not his mouth.

Ez. 3:2   So I opened my mouth and he gave me the scroll to eat.

Ez. 37:13-14   Then you shall know that I am the LORD, when I open your graves and have you rise from them, O my people! I will put my spirit in you that you may live, and I will settle you upon your land; thus you shall know that I am the Lord. I have promised, and I will do it, says the Lord.

Mal. 3:10   Bring the whole tithe / into the storehouse, / That there may be food in my house, / and try me in this, says the Lord of hosts: / Shall I not open for you the floodgates of heaven, / to pour down blessing upon you without measure?

Matt. 2:11   ... and on entering the house, they saw the child with Mary his mother. They prostrated themselves and did him homage. Then they opened their treasures and offered him gifts of gold, frankincense, and myrrh.

Matt. 7:7	Ask and it will be given to you; seek and you will find; knock and the door will be opened to you.
Matt. 7:8	For everyone who asks, receives; and the one who seeks, finds; and to the one who knocks, the door will be opened.
Matt. 9:29-30	Then he touched their eyes and said, "Let it be done to you according to your faith." And their eyes were opened.
Matt. 20:32-33	"What do you want me to do for you?" They answered him, "Lord, let our eyes be opened."
Mk. 1:10-11	On coming up out of the water he saw the heavens being torn open and the Spirit, like a dove, descending upon him. And a voice came from the heavens, "You are my beloved Son; with you I am well pleased."
Mk. 7:34	Then he looked up to heaven and groaned, and said to him, "*Ephphatha!*" (that is, "Be opened!")
Lk. 12:35-36	Gird your loins and light your lamps and be like servants who await their master's return from a wedding, ready to open immediately when he comes and knocks.
Lk. 24:30-31	He took bread, said the blessing, broke it and gave it to them. With that their eyes were opened and they recognized him.
Lk. 24:32	Were not our hearts burning [within us] while he spoke to us on the way and opened the scriptures to us?
Lk. 24:45	Then he opened their minds to understand the scriptures.

Jn. 10:3	The gatekeeper opens it for him, and the sheep hear his voice, as he calls his own sheep by name and leads them out.
Acts 26:17-18	I shall deliver you from this people and from the Gentiles to whom I send you, to open their eyes that they may turn from darkness to light and from the power of Satan to God, so that they may obtain forgiveness of sins and an inheritance among those who have been consecrated by faith in me.
2Cor. 6:13	Be open yourselves.
Eph. 6:19-20	… that speech may be given me to open my mouth, to make known with boldness the mystery of the gospel … so that I may have the courage to speak as I must.
Col. 4:3	At the same time, pray for us, too, that God may open a door to us for the word, to speak of the mystery of Christ.
Rev. 3:8	I know your works (behold, I have left an open door before you, which no one can close).
Rev. 3:20	Behold, I stand at the door and knock. If anyone hears my voice and opens the door, [then] I will enter his house and dine with him, and he with me.

PATIENCE

Let nothing disturb thee;
Let nothing dismay thee;
All things pass;
God never changes.
Patience attains
All that it strives for.
He who has God
Finds he lacks nothing;
God alone suffices.

St. Teresa of Avila

PATIENCE

Patience ... a virtue all want, but struggle in the practice. I used to pray for patience. I hoped God would simply fill me with patience; however, that is not the way God works. Rather, I discovered that God was going to help me *develop* patience ... through the daily opportunity to practice the art of ... being patient! For me, patience is difficult because it involves dying to myself, my way, my timing, and my desires!

Once, when I was asked to define patience, I replied, "Patience is waiting in love." It was a completely spontaneous answer that came to my lips so easily. To use patience, means to wait in love, to wait in quiet and calm, believing that all will be well ... waiting in faith! Sometimes, "waiting in love" calls us to practice love in ... forgiveness!

I will try to remember this the next time the traffic is in a jam or I am stuck in a slow line at the supermarket. Or perhaps I'll remember when the two year old is trying to explore the world, or the teenager is trying to grow up; or an elderly person is struggling with asking for help, but everything I offer is wrong.

A true gardener would be someone who is patient. They know that the soil has to be prepared, seeds sown, nurtured with water and the right light. And then they wait! They trust that all will be well. Their patient attentiveness will bring about great beauty when the seeds come to maturity and bear blossoms or fruit.

The word patience is like a seed sown into our very soul. Perhaps, we should simply be kind, as we wait for patience to fully blossom within us. Lord, you are the Master Gardener, may we simply trust in you and be patient with ourselves!

Reflection Questions:

How would you define patience?
How does dying to yourself help you to become more patient?

213

PATIENCE

Job 6:11 What strength have I that I should endure, / and what is my limit that I should be patient?

Pro. 14:29 The patient man shows much good sense.

Pro. 15:18 An ill-tempered man stirs up strife, / but a patient man allays discord.

Pro. 16:32 A patient man is better than a warrior, / and he who rules his temper, than he who takes a city.

Pro. 25:15 By patience is a ruler persuaded, / and a soft tongue will break a bone.

Ecc. 7:8 Better is the end of speech than its beginning; / better is the patient spirit than the lofty spirit.

Sir. 1:20 A patient man need stand firm but for a time, / and then contentment comes back to him.

Sir. 2:4-5 Accept whatever befalls you, / in crushing misfortune be patient. / For in fire gold is tested, / and worthy men in the crucible of humiliation.

Dan. 12:12 Blessed is the man who has patience and perseveres.

Acts 26:3 I beg you to listen patiently.

Rom. 2:4 Or do you hold his priceless kindness, forbearance, and patience in low esteem, unaware that the kindness of God would lead you to repentance?

Gal. 5:22-23 The fruit of the Spirit is love, joy, peace, patience, kindness, generosity, faithfulness, gentleness, self-control.

Eph. 4:1-2 I, then, a prisoner of the Lord, urge you to live in a manner worthy of the call you have received, with all humility and gentleness, with patience, bearing with one another through love.

Col. 1:10-11 ... to live in a manner worthy of the Lord so as to be fully pleasing, in every good work bearing fruit and growing in the knowledge of God, strengthened with every power, in accord with his glorious might, for all endurance and patience, with joy.

Col. 3:12 Put on then, as God's chosen ones, holy and beloved, heartfelt compassion, kindness, humility, gentleness, and patience.

1Thes. 5:14 We urge you, ... admonish the idle, cheer the fainthearted, support the weak, be patient with all.

1Tim. 6:11 Pursue righteousness, devotion, faith, love, patience, and gentleness.

2Tim. 4:2 ... proclaim the word; be persistent whether it is convenient or inconvenient; convince, reprimand, encourage through all patience and teaching.

Heb. 5:2 He is able to deal patiently with the ignorant and erring, for he himself is beset by weakness.

Heb. 6:15 And so, after patient waiting, he obtained the promise.

Ja. 5:7-9	Be patient, therefore, … until the coming of the Lord. See how the farmer waits for the precious fruit of the earth, being patient with it until it receives the early and the late rains. You too must be patient.
1Pet. 2:20	But what credit is there if you are patient when beaten for doing wrong? But if you are patient when you suffer for doing what is good, this is grace before God.
2Pet. 3:9	The Lord does not delay his promise, as some regard "delay," but he is patient with you, not wishing that any should perish but that all should come to repentance.
2Pet. 3:15	And consider the patience of our Lord as salvation, as our beloved brother Paul, according to the wisdom given to him, also wrote to you.

PEACE

Imagine all the people living life in peace.
You may say I'm a dreamer,
But I'm not the only one.
I hope someday you'll join us and
The world will live as one.

John Lennon

PEACE

Peace is not the absence of chaos & stress. I have come to discover that peace is the quieting presence of Christ, in the midst of it all. If you watch someone who has this gift of peace, no matter what troubles beset them; you will notice how they seem to have a quiet joy that sustains them. For so long I yearned to have that peace.

Peace does not come easy. When I am not at peace, I know that I am not in harmony with life. I am more like a wheel out of balance trying to travel smoothly down the road. How do I find that center, that harmony once more? Prayer brings me back into harmony with Christ! Is this why Jesus kept slipping away to a quiet place? Is this where Jesus found His peace? I too, must slip away to a quiet place where no one can find me. Okay, in my family home that is in the bathroom … door locked! Don't laugh. We do what we can!

Imagine a balance beam, such as the gymnasts use, then, imagine yourself staying centered and balanced on that beam … that is me trying to stay in peace! It doesn't take much to move any of us out of balance. A harsh word, anxiety, fear, anger, and even just the problems that crop up in everyday life can make me fall off. Too little sleep, too much stress and off I go. Simply being aware of this "balancing act" helps me immensely. As soon as I am aware that I am moving "out of peace" I immediately act to stay centered. Focusing on my every breath slows me down and helps me to choose to forgive, to let go or whatever it takes to stay balanced. Peace is a choice we can all make.

For true peace in the world to come about, I must start with myself. Because if I am at peace with me, then I will be more at peace with others and God. Maybe, just maybe, we will truly bring the world to peace … one person, one home, one community at a time until the peace of Christ truly reigns!

Patti King

Reflection Questions:

What needs to change within yourself to live in peace?

Where do you go to come to peace?

PEACE

Num. 6:24-26   The LORD bless you and keep you! / The LORD let his face shine upon you, and be gracious to you! / The Lord look upon you kindly and give you peace!

Ps. 4:9   In peace I shall both lie down and sleep, / for you alone, LORD, make me secure.

Ps. 34:15   Turn from evil and do good; / seek peace and pursue it.

Ps. 85:9   I will listen for the word of God; / surely the LORD will proclaim peace / To his people, to the faithful, / to those who trust in him.

Ps. 85:11   Love and truth will meet; / justice and peace will kiss.

Ps. 119:165   Lovers of your teaching have much peace; / for them there is no stumbling block.

Pro. 3:17   Her ways are pleasant ways, / and all her paths are peace.

Pro. 12:20   Those who counsel peace have joy.

Ecc. 3:8   A time to love, and a time to hate; / a time of war, and a time of peace.

Sir. 26:2   A worthy wife brings joy to her husband, / peaceful and full is his life.

Sir. 50:23   May he grant you joy of heart / and may peace abide among you.

Is. 32:17   Justice will bring about peace; / right will produce calm and security.

Is. 32:18   My people will live in peaceful country, / in secure dwellings and quiet resting places.

Is. 52:7   How beautiful upon the mountains /are the feet of him who brings glad tidings, / Announcing peace, bearing good news, / announcing salvation, and saying to Zion, / "Your God is King."

Is. 54:10   Though the mountains leave their place /and the hills be shaken, / My love shall never leave you / nor my covenant of peace be shaken, / says the Lord, who has mercy on you.

Is. 55:12   Yes, in joy you shall depart, / in peace you shall be brought back; / Mountains and hills shall break out in song before you, / and all the trees of the countryside shall clap their hands.

Jer. 33:6   Behold, I will treat and assuage the city's wounds; I will heal them, and reveal to them an abundance of lasting peace.

Ez. 37:26   I will make with them a covenant of peace, it shall be an everlasting covenant with them, and I will multiply them, and put my sanctuary among them forever.

Zech. 8:16-17   These then are the things you should do: speak the truth to one another; let there be honesty and peace in the judgments at your gates, and let none of you plot evil against another in his heart, nor love a false oath.

Mal. 2:5   My covenant with him was one of life and peace

Matt. 5:9	Blessed are the peacemakers, / for they will be called children of God.
Mk. 5:34	Daughter, your faith has saved you. Go in peace and be cured of your affliction.
Mk. 9:49-50	Everyone will be salted with fire. Salt is good, if salt becomes insipid, with what will you restore its flavor? Keep salt in yourselves and you will have peace with one another.
Lk. 1:79	… to shine on those who sit in darkness and death's shadow, / to guide our feet into the path of peace.
Lk. 2:14	Glory to God in the highest /and on earth peace to those on whom his favor rests.
Lk. 7:50	But he said to the woman, "You faith has saved you; go in peace."
Jn. 14:27	Peace I leave with you: my peace I give to you. Not as the world gives do I give it you. Do not let your hearts be troubled.
Jn. 16:33	I have told you this so that you might have peace in me. In the world you will have trouble, but take courage, I have conquered the world.
Jn. 20:21	Peace be with you. As the Father has sent me, so I send you.
Rom. 1:7	Grace to you and peace from God our Father and the Lord Jesus Christ.
Rom. 2:10	There will be glory, honor, and peace for everyone who does good.

Rom. 5:1   Therefore, since we have been justified by faith, we have peace with God through our Lord Jesus Christ.

Rom. 12:18   If possible, on your part, live at peace with all.

Rom. 14:17   For the kingdom of God is not a matter of food and drink, but of righteousness, peace, and joy in the holy Spirit.

Rom. 15:13   May the God of hope fill you with all joy and peace in believing, so that you may abound in hope by the power of the holy Spirit.

1Cor. 7:15   God has called you to peace.

2Cor. 13:11   Finally, brothers, rejoice. Mend your ways, encourage one another, agree with one another, live in peace, and the God of love and peace will be with you.

Gal. 5:22-23 The fruit of the Spirit is love, joy, peace, patience, kindness, generosity, faithfulness, gentleness, self-control.

Eph. 4:1-3   Live in a manner worthy of the call you have received, with all humility and gentleness, with patience, bearing with one another through love, striving to preserve the unity of the spirit through the bond of peace.

Eph. 6:13-15 Therefore, put on the armor of God ... So stand fast with your loins girded in truth, clothed with righteousness as a breastplate, and your feet shod in readiness for the gospel of peace.

Phil. 4:6-7	Have no anxiety at all, but in everything, by prayer and petition, with thanksgiving, make your requests known to God. Then the peace of God that surpasses all understanding will guard your hearts and minds in Christ Jesus.
Col. 3:15	Let the peace of Christ control your hearts, the peace into which you were also called in one body.
1Th. 5:13	Be at peace among yourselves.
1Th. 5:23-24	May the God of peace himself make you perfectly holy and may you entirely, spirit, soul, and body, be preserved blameless for the coming of our Lord Jesus Christ.
2Th. 3:16	May the Lord of peace himself give you peace at all times and in every way.
Heb. 12:14	Strive for peace with everyone, and for that holiness without which no one will see the Lord.
Heb. 13:20-21	May the God of peace … furnish you with all that is good, that you may do his will. May he carry out in you what is pleasing to him through Jesus Christ.
Ja. 3:18	The fruit of righteousness is sown in peace for those who cultivate peace.
2Pet. 1:2	May grace and peace be yours in abundance through knowledge of God and of Jesus our Lord.
2Jn. 3	Grace, mercy, and peace will be with us from God the Father and from Jesus Christ the Father's Son in truth and love.

PRAYER

It is not enough to say prayers,
one must be prayer,
one should not offer what one has,
but what one is.

Paul Evdokimov

PRAYER

What does it mean to "pray?" When I was a child, it meant knowing "word prayers" like the Our Father. At that time to pray meant ..."Okay, Lord, here I am, listen to me, please!" Then, as I grew older, I experienced the difficulties of life. Prayer took on a greater meaning in my life. "Lord, I'm in deep trouble, help me and I promise whatever it takes!" I found myself "giving God directions" as to how my prayer should be answered. Like I know what is best ... Ha!

The good thing (and there is a good thing) about growing older, is that eventually wisdom begins to take hold. Thank the Lord that I came to my senses and realized that I do not know best. My definition of prayer changed for me:

Prayer is the loving relationship between God and me.
As in most loving relationships,
more happens and is exchanged with no words!
It is sacred time that I spend with the One Who Loves Me.
I bring my concerns to God and let God decide how to answer.
Simply, I dwell in God's love.

I found meditation and contemplative prayer like golden gateways to a place where I could truly come into God's presence! My deepest prayer times are now when God and I just gaze at each other or we gaze upon creation together in love! It really doesn't matter what kind of prayer one chooses. What is important is that you open your heart to God and that God is always there waiting for you ... the one God loves!

David Kauffman, a gifted songwriter whose voice helps to lift my heart in prayer, says in one of his songs titled, "I Will Make This Day My Prayer:"

"I will make this day my prayer.
I will give you everything
that I am and do today."

And we people say ....**AMEN!**

Reflection Questions:

* How did you pray as a child?
* How has your prayer changed through the years?
* Where is your favorite place to pray?
* What needs to change in you that you may be more open to "growing in a more prayerful relationship" with the One Who Loves you?

PRAYER

2Ki. 20:5   I have heard your prayer and seen your tears. I will heal you.

2Chr. 6:40   My God, may your eyes be open and your ears attentive to the prayer of this place.

2Chr. 7:14   If my people, upon whom my name has been pronounced, humble themselves and pray, and seek my presence and turn from their evil ways, I will hear them from heaven and pardon their sins and revive their land.

Neh. 1:11   O LORD, may your ear be attentive to my prayer and that of all your willing servants who revere your name. Grant success to your servant this day.

Tobit 12:8   Prayer and fasting are good, but better than either is almsgiving accompanied by righteousness.

Ps. 4:2   Answer when I call, my saving God. / In my troubles, you cleared a way; / show me favor; hear my prayer.

Ps. 17:6   I call upon you; answer me, O God. / Turn your ear to me; hear my prayer.

Ps. 20:6   May we shout for joy at your victory, / raise the banners in the name of our God. / The Lord grant your every prayer!

Ps. 21:3   You have granted him his heart's desire; / you did not refuse the prayer of his lips.

Ps. 66:19-20	God did hear / and listened to my voice in prayer. / Blessed be God, who did not refuse me / the kindness I sought in prayer.
Ps. 69:14	But I pray to you, LORD, / for the time of your favor. / God, in your great kindness answer me / with your constant help.
Ps. 88:2-3	LORD, my God, I call out by day; / at night I cry aloud in your presence. / Let my prayer come before you; / incline your ear to my cry!
Ps. 107:1-2	"Give thanks to the LORD who is good, / whose love endures forever!" / Let that be the prayer of the Lord's redeemed.
Ps. 140:7	I say to the LORD: You are my God; / listen, LORD, to the words of my prayer.
Ps. 141:2	Let my prayer be incense before you; / my uplifted hands an evening sacrifice.
Ps. 143:1	LORD, hear my prayer; / in your faithfulness listen to my pleading; / answer me in your justice.
Wis. 7:7	Therefore I prayed, and prudence was given me; / I pleaded and the spirit of Wisdom came to me.
Sir. 28:2	Forgive your neighbor's injustice; / then when you pray, your own sins will be forgiven.
Sir. 37:15	Pray to God / to set your feet in the path of truth.
Sir. 51:11	I will ever praise your name / and be constant in my prayers to you; / Thereupon the Lord heard my voice, / he listened to my appeal.

Jer. 29:12	When you call me, when you go to pray to me, I will listen to you.
Matt. 5:44	But I say to you, love your enemies, and pray for those who persecute you.
Matt. 6:6	But when you pray, go to your inner room, close the door, and pray to your Father in secret, and your Father who sees in secret will repay you.
Matt. 6:7, 9	In praying, do not babble like the pagans, who think that they will be heard because of their many words. … This is how you are to pray: … Our Father …
Matt. 21:22	Whatever you ask for in prayer with faith, you will receive.
Matt. 26:41	Watch and pray that you may not undergo the test. The spirit is willing, but the flesh is weak.
Mk. 11:25	When you stand to pray, forgive anyone against whom you have a grievance, so that your heavenly Father may in turn forgive you your transgressions.
Lk. 6:27-28	But to you who hear I say, love your enemies, do good to those who hate you, bless those who curse you, pray for those who mistreat you.
Lk. 21:36	Be vigilant at all times and pray that you have the strength to escape the tribulations that are imminent and to stand before the Son of Man.
Lk. 22:32	But I have prayed that your own faith may not fail; and once you have turned back, you must strengthen your brothers.
Jn. 17:20	I pray not only for them, but also for those who will believe in me through their word.

Acts 1:14	All these devoted themselves with one accord to prayer.
Acts 4:31	As they prayed, the place where they were gathered shook and they were all filled with the holy Spirit and continued to speak the word of God with boldness.
Rom. 8:26	In the same way, the Spirit too comes to the aid of our weakness; for we do not know how to pray as we ought, but the Spirit itself intercedes with inexpressible groanings.
Rom. 12:12	Rejoice in hope, endure in affliction, persevere in prayer.
Eph. 6:18	With all prayer and supplication, pray at every opportunity in the Spirit.
Phil. 1:3-4	I give thanks to my God at every remembrance of you, praying always with joy in my every prayer for all of you.
Phil. 1:9-10	And this is my prayer: that your love may increase ever more and more in knowledge and every kind of perception to discern what is of value, so that you may be pure and blameless for the day of Christ.
Phil. 4:6-7	Have no anxiety at all, but in everything by prayer and petition, with thanksgiving, make your requests known to God. Then the peace of God that surpasses all understanding will guard your hearts and minds in Christ Jesus.
Col. 1:3	We always give thanks to God, the Father of our Lord Jesus Christ, when we pray for you, for we have heard of your faith in Christ Jesus and the love that you have for all the holy ones.

Col. 1:9	We do not cease praying for you and asking that you may be filled with the knowledge of his will through all spiritual wisdom and understanding.
Col. 4:2	Persevere in prayer, being watchful in it with thanksgiving.
1Th. 1:2-4	We give thanks to God always for all of you, remembering you in our prayers, unceasingly calling to mind your work of faith and labor of love and endurance in hope of our Lord Jesus Christ … knowing, brothers, loved by God, how you were chosen.
2Th. 1:11	To this end, we always pray for you, that our God may make you worthy of his calling and powerfully bring to fulfillment every good purpose and every effort of faith.
1Tim. 2:8	It is my wish, then, that in every place the men should pray, lifting up holy hands, without anger or argument.
1Tim 4:4-5	For everything created by God is good, and nothing is to be rejected when received with thanksgiving, for it is made holy by the invocation of God in prayer.
Ja. 5:14-15	Is anyone among you sick? He should summon the presbyters of the church, and they should pray over him and anoint [him] with oil in the name of the Lord, and the prayer of faith will save the sick person, and the Lord will raise him up.
Ja. 5:16	The fervent prayer of a righteous person is very powerful.

PRECIOUS

Each child is a reminder
of how precious life is for us all.
Do not neglect the child within
that yearns to live fully.

Patti King

PRECIOUS

What is "precious?" Something valuable? In this day and time of a throw away society, what might be considered truly precious? To each individual it may mean something different. Only you can answer that. We often put our faith in gold, money, power, fame and possessions ... and we call them precious. But do they bring us what we truly desire? What of health, family and faith? If I see these as precious, does it show in my life?

My health ... Do I live in a healthy manner?

My family ... Do I give them special time to build this relationship?

My faith ... Do I spend quality time in prayer and devotion?

One day on a weekend women's retreat, our retreat leader proclaimed Is. 43:4 ...

> Because you are precious in my eyes
> and glorious, and because I love you!

That day I really heard that passage! Maybe it was the soft afternoon light, the quiet room, or even the voice of our sacred retreat leader, who I call, AMMA. But something in me opened, changed and took root! Before that day, I never considered myself as being precious or being precious to God. However, after that day, I saw myself in a whole new light. God would not sell me or betray me. God created me ... God's precious creation. My journey of self discovery began in earnest. Strangely, this new knowledge changed my perspective of seeing everyone else! All are precious in God's sight!

Oh, I know, some people try really hard to cover up their "precious self," but it is for us to look a little harder, and love a little more. Just like God does for us!

Reflection Questions:

What is precious to you?

Do you see yourself as the precious child of God?

PRECIOUS

Job 28:10-11   … his eyes behold all that is precious. / He probes the wellsprings of the streams, / and brings hidden things to light.

Ps. 35:17   LORD, how long will you look on? / Save me from roaring beasts, / my precious life from lions!

Ps. 36:8   How precious is your love, O God! / We take refuge in the shadow of your wings.

Ps. 119:72   Teaching from your lips is more precious to me / than heaps of silver and gold.

Ps. 133:1-2   How good it is, how pleasant / where the people dwell as one! / Like precious ointment on the head, / running down upon the beard …

Ps. 139:17   How precious to me are your designs, O God; / how vast the sum of them!

Pro. 3:13, 15   Happy the man who finds wisdom, / the man who gains understanding. / She is more precious than corals, / and none of your choice possessions can compare with her.

Pro. 20:15   Like gold or a wealth of corals, / wise lips are a precious ornament.

Pro. 21:20   Precious treasure remains in the house of the wise.

Pro. 24:3-4   By wisdom is a house built, / by understanding is it made firm; / And by knowledge are its rooms filled / with every precious and pleasing possession

Sir. 30:15   More precious than gold is health and well being, / contentment of spirit than coral.

Is. 28:16   See, I am laying a stone in Zion, / a stone that has been tested, / A precious cornerstone as a sure foundation; / he who puts his faith in it shall not be shaken.

Is. 43:4   Because you are precious in my eyes / and glorious, and because I love you.

Jer. 15:19   If you repent, so that I restore you, / in my presence you shall stand; / If you bring forth the precious without the vile, / you shall be my mouthpiece.

Ez. 28:13   In Eden, the garden of God, you were, / and every precious stone was your covering; / ... Of gold your pendants and jewels / were made, on the day you were created.

Ja. 5:7-8   Be patient, therefore, brothers, until the coming of the Lord. See how the farmer waits for the precious fruit of the earth, being patient with it until it receives the early and late rains. You too must be patient. Make your hearts firm, because the coming of the Lord is at hand.

1Pet. 1:6-7   In this you rejoice, although now for a little while you may have to suffer through various trials, so that the genuineness of your faith, more precious than gold, ... may prove to be for praise, glory, and honor at the revelation of Jesus Christ.

1Pet. 2:4   Come to him, a living stone, rejected by human beings but chosen and precious in the sight of God.

1Pet. 2:5-6   Like living stones, let yourselves be built into a spiritual house to be a holy priesthood to offer spiritual sacrifices acceptable to God through Jesus Christ. For it says in scripture: / "Behold, I am laying a stone in Zion, / a cornerstone, chosen and precious, / and whoever believes in it shall not be put to shame."

1Pet. 3:3-4   Your adornment [should be] … the hidden character of the heart, expressed in the imperishable beauty of a gentle and calm disposition, which is precious in the sight of God.

2Pet. 1:4   He has bestowed on us the precious and very great promises, so that through them you may come to share in the divine nature.

SEEK

Show me, O Lord, your mercy,
and delight my heart with it.
Let me find you,
whom I seek so longingly.

St. Jerome

SEEK

Seek ... a word that denotes action or movement towards something or someone. Remember the times when we were seeking the others in hide and seek? With great anticipation we never gave up. We looked in every nook and cranny. To seek was a joyful activity, for we loved treasure hunting. Sometimes, we were the one being sought and we hid as well as we could.

What do we seek as adults? Do we seek fame and fortune? Perfection in ourselves? Perfect homes? Perfect families? Faithful friends? Or do we have the wisdom to seek that which will fill our deepest desires ... God? Sometimes our best teachers are the little ones. On an ordinary day a small delightful toddler taught me a new way of seeing the word ... seek.

Sitting on a porch listening to a precious young mother talk about her day, this little blond headed boy quietly stayed behind his mother. With no notice, he would "sneak a peak" and dash back in safety. I really tried to listen to the Mom, but this little one kept quietly distracting me. I made the decision to be attentive to his Mom, when from behind her the most beautiful smile came forth and eyes so full of delightful joy that he had my heart and attention! And at that moment, I felt God's presence! God's simple Joy! God's radiant Love!

I was being sought! God was seeking me out all along! I only had to be still enough to be aware of the awesome presence of God! You see with God we may be the ones hiding from the very Presence that will fill the desire of our hearts. And we hide so well. Thankfully, God is a great seeker and never gives up!

Let the One who seeks you ... find you!

Reflection Questions:

What or who do you seek?

At this time are you more of the seeker or the one hiding? Why?

What difference does it make to you to know that God is seeking you?

SEEK

Deut. 4:29   Yet there too you shall seek the LORD, your God; and you shall indeed find him when you search after him with your whole heart and your whole soul.

1Chr. 16:11   Look to the LORD in his strength; / seek to serve him constantly.

1Chr. 22:19   Devote your hearts and souls to seeking the LORD your God.

1Chr. 28:9   As for you, Solomon, my son, know the God of your father and serve him with a perfect heart and a willing soul, for the Lord searches all hearts and understands all the mind's thoughts. If you seek him, he will let himself be found by you.

2 Chr. 7:14   If my people, upon whom my name has been pronounced, humble themselves and pray, and seek my presence and turn from their evil ways, I will hear them from heaven and pardon their sins and revive their land.

Ps. 9:11   Those who honor your name trust in you: / you never forsake those who seek you, Lord.

Ps. 27:4   One thing I ask of the LORD; / this I seek: / To dwell in the LORD's house / all the days of my life.

Ps. 27:8   "Come," says my heart, "seek God's face"; / your face, LORD, do I seek!

Ps. 34:5   I sought the LORD, who answered me, / delivered me from all my fears.

Ps. 34:15	Turn from evil and do good; / seek peace and pursue it.
Ps. 40:17	May all who seek you / rejoice and be glad in you. / May those who long for your help / always say, "The Lord be glorified."
Ps. 57:2	Have mercy on me, God, / have mercy on me. / In you I seek shelter, / in the shadow of your wings I seek shelter / till harm pass by.
Ps. 69:33	"See, you lowly ones, and be glad; / you who seek God, take heart!"
Ps. 105:3	Glory in his holy name; / rejoice, O hearts that seek the Lord!
Ps. 105:4	Rely on the mighty Lord; / constantly seek his face.
Ps. 119:176	I have wandered like a lost sheep; / seek out your servant, / for I do not forget your commands.
Wis. 1:1	Love justice, you who judge the earth; / think of the Lord in goodness; / and seek him in integrity of heart.
Wis. 6:12	Resplendent and unfading is Wisdom, / and she is readily perceived by those who love her, / and found by those who seek her.
Sir. 6:28-29	Search her out, discover her; seek her and you will find her. / Then when you have her, do not let her go; / Thus you will afterward find rest in her, / and she will become your joy! (wisdom)

Sir. 39:6   His care is to seek the Lord, his Maker, / to petition the Most High, / To open his lips in prayer, / to ask pardon for his sins. / Then, if it pleases the Lord Almighty, / he will be filled with the spirit of understanding: / He will pour forth his words of wisdom / and in prayer give thanks to the Lord.

Is. 51:1   Listen to me, you who pursue justice; / who seek the Lord; / Look to the rock from which you were hewn, / to the pit from which / you were quarried.

Is. 55:6   Seek the Lord while he may be found, / call him while he is near.

Jer. 29:13-14   When you look for me, you will find me. Yes, when you seek me with all your heart, you will find me with you, says the Lord, and I will change your lot.

Lam. 3:25   Good is the Lord to one who waits for him, / to the soul that seeks him.

Ez. 34:15-16   I myself will pasture my sheep; I myself will give them rest, says the Lord God. The lost will seek out, the strayed I will bring back, the injured I will bind up, the sick I will heal.

Amos 5:14   Seek good and not evil, / that you may live; / Then truly will the Lord, the God of hosts, / be with you as you claim!

Zeph. 2:3   Seek the Lord, all you humble of the earth, / who have observed his law; / Seek justice, seek humility; / perhaps you may be sheltered / on the day of the Lord's anger.

Matt. 6:33   Seek first the kingdom [of God] and his righteousness, and all these things will be given you besides.

Matt. 7:7   Ask and it will be given to you; seek and you will find; knock and the door will be opened to you.

Matt. 18:12   If a man has a hundred sheep and one of them goes astray, will he not leave the ninety-nine in the hills and go search of the stray?

Lk. 12:29, 31   As for you, do not seek what you are to eat and what you are to drink, and do not worry anymore. Instead, seek his kingdom, and these other things will be given you besides.

Lk. 17:33   Whoever seeks to preserve his life will lose it, but whoever loses it will save it.

Jn. 4:23   But the hour is coming, and is now here, when true worshipers will worship the Father in Spirit and truth; and indeed the Father seeks such people to worship him.

Jn. 7:18   Whoever speaks on his own seeks his own glory, but whoever seeks the glory of the one who sent him is truthful, and there is no wrong in him.

Rom. 8:27   And the one who searches hearts knows what is the intention of the Spirit, because it intercedes for the holy ones according to God's will.

1Cor. 10:24   No one should seek his own advantage, but that of his neighbor.

1Cor. 13:4-5   Love is patient, love is kind. It is not jealous, [love] is not pompous, it is not inflated, it is not rude, it does not seek its own interests, it is not quick-tempered, it does not brood over injury.

1Cor. 14:12   So with yourselves: since you strive eagerly for spirits, seek to have an abundance of them for building up the church.

Gal. 1:10   Am I now currying favor with human beings or God? Or am I seeking to please people? If I were still trying to please people, I would not be a slave of Christ.

1Thes. 5:15   See that no one returns evil for evil; rather, always seek what is good [both] for each other and for all.

1Pet. 3:11   Seek peace and follow after it.

SERVANT

To give oneself as a servant for God
is like a thread in the hand of the Master Weaver;
who weaves our strength and beauty
into the tapestry of God's creation.

Patti King

SERVANT

A "servant" is one who serves or assists another. But in this world, at this time, being a servant is not the desirable occupation. In fact, most of us, probably desire to have others serve us! Yet, in the scriptures we find that is exactly what Jesus asks of us ... to serve one another!

To serve another means that I must place the needs and welfare of the others before myself. Easy to say, but not easy to live, as I have found out over the years. Just ask a young mother who has stayed up all night with a sick child. Yet she still gets up in the morning to serve her family breakfast and get them off for the day. Or the father who worked all day and comes home to listen to his children and then continues with chores.

During the summer, when school is out, I used to take my two daughters to their great Grandmother's to help her out. Now those two precious girls were gems, and what they discovered was very important. You might step out in faith and love to serve someone, but you receive so much more from the experience. We would watch a sometimes bitter, frustrated woman become transformed in our visit! Our serving in love and joy really made a difference. Without realizing it, we were being transformed as well!

Responding to the love of God, and to serve as God's servant, is a privilege and a gift. Following Jesus' example at the Last Supper, washing the disciples feet, is what each of us should try to imitate. However, we must serve in love, and with joy if we want to reflect Jesus. Try it, you'll never be the same again!

Reflection Questions

Reflect upon a time when Jesus called you to be a servant.

1. Describe this time, how did you feel?
2. What did it cost you?
3. How did your serving, show the love of Christ?
4. How did you feel after this time of serving?

SERVANT

Deut. 10:12   What does the LORD, your God, ask of you but to fear the LORD, your God, and follow his ways exactly, to love and serve the Lord, your God, with all your heart and all your soul.

Jos. 24:15   Decide today whom you will serve. ... As for me and my household, we will serve the Lord.

Ruth 2:13   May I prove worthy of your kindness, my lord; you have comforted me, your servant, with your consoling words, would indeed that I were a servant of yours!

ISam. 3:9   Speak, LORD, for your servant is listening.

1Ki. 3:9   Give your servant, therefore, an understanding heart to judge your people and to distinguish right from wrong.

1Chr. 28:9   As for you, Solomon, my son, know the God of your father and serve him with a perfect heart and a willing soul, for the Lord searches all hearts and understands all the mind's thoughts.

Judith 16:14   Let your every creature serve you; / for you spoke, and they were made, / You sent forth your spirit, and they were created; / no one can resist your word.

Ps. 31:17   Let your face shine on your servant; / save me in your kindness.

Ps. 86:4   Gladden the soul of your servant; / to you, Lord, I lift up my soul.

Ps. 89:21	I have chosen David, my servant; / with my holy oil I have anointed him.
Ps. 119:17	Be kind to your servant that I may live, / that I may keep your word.
Ps. 119:49	Remember your word to your servant / by which you give me hope.
Ps. 119:65	You have treated your servant well, / according to your word, O Lord.
Ps. 119:76	May your love comfort me / in accord with your promise to your servant.
Ps. 119:124	Act with kindness toward your servant; / teach me your laws.
Ps. 119:125	I am your servant; give me discernment / that I may know your decrees.
Ps. 119:135	Let your face shine upon your servant; / teach me your laws.
Ps. 119:140	Your servant loves your promise; / it has been proved by fire.
Ps. 119:176	I have wandered like a lost sheep; / seek out your servant, / for I do not forget your commands.
Ps. 123:1-2	To you, I raise my eyes, / to you enthroned in heaven. / Yes, like the eyes of a servant / on the hand of his master, / Like the eyes of a maid / on the hand of her mistress. / So our eyes are on the Lord our God, / till we are shown favor.
Sir. 2:1	My son, when you come to serve the Lord, / prepare yourself for trials.

Sir. 35:16	He who serves God willingly is heard; / his petition reaches the heavens.
Is. 41:9-10	You whom I have called my servant, / whom I have chosen and will not cast off — / Fear not, I am with you; / be not dismayed; I am your God. / I will strengthen you, and help you, / and uphold you with my right hand of justice.
Is. 42:1	Here is my servant whom I uphold, / my chosen one with whom I am pleased, / Upon whom I have put my spirit; / he shall bring forth justice to the nations.
Is. 43:10	You are my witnesses, says the LORD, / my servants whom I have chosen / To know and believe in me / and understand that it is I.
Is. 44:1-2	Hear then, O Jacob, my servant, / Israel, whom I have chosen. / Thus says the LORD who made you, / your help, who formed you from the womb; / Fear not, O Jacob, my servant, / the darling whom I have chosen.
Is. 44:21-22	Remember this, O Jacob, / you, O Israel, who are my servant! / I formed you to be a servant to me; / O Israel, by me you shall never be forgotten: / I have brushed away your offenses like a cloud, / your sins like a mist; / return to me, for I have redeemed you.
Is. 49:3	You are my servant, ... / through whom I show my glory.
Is. 49:5	For now the LORD has spoken / who formed me as his servant from the womb, / That Jacob may be brought back to him / and Israel gathered to him; / And I am made glorious in the sight of the Lord, and my God is now my strength!

Is. 49:6   It is too little, he says, for you to be my servant, / to raise up the tribes of Jacob, / and restore the survivors of Israel; / I will make you a light to the nations, / that my salvation may reach to the ends of the earth.

Is. 53:11   Because of his affliction / he shall see the light in fullness of days; / Through his suffering, my servant shall justify many, / and their guilt he shall bear.

Jer. 30:10   But you, my servant Jacob, fear not, says the LORD, / be not dismayed, O Israel! / Behold, I will deliver you from the far-off land, / your descendants, from their land of exile; / Jacob shall again find rest, / shall be tranquil and undisturbed.

Matt. 8:8   "Lord, I am not worthy to have you enter under my roof; only say the word and my servant will be healed."

Matt. 12:18   "Behold, my servant whom I have chosen, / my beloved in whom I delight; / I shall place my spirit upon him, / and he will proclaim justice to the Gentiles."

Matt. 20:26-27   Whoever wishes to be great among you shall be your servant; whoever wishes to be first among you shall be your slave.

Matt. 23:11-12   The greatest among you must be your servant. Whoever exalts himself will be humbled; but whoever humbles himself will be exalted.

Matt. 25:23   "Well done, my good and faithful servant. Since you were faithful in small matters, I will give you great responsibilities. Come, share your master's joy."

Mk. 9:35   If anyone wishes to be first, he shall be the last of all and the servant of all.

Lk. 2:29   Now, Master, you may let your servant go / in peace, according to your word.

Lk. 12:35-36   Gird your loins and light your lamps and be like servants who await their master's return from a wedding, ready to open immediately when he comes and knocks.

Lk. 16:13   No servant can serve two masters. He will either hate one and love the other, or be devoted to one and despise the other.

Jn. 12:26   Whoever serves me must follow me, and where I am, there also will my servant be. The Father will honor whoever serves me.

Acts 4:29   Enable your servants to speak your word with all boldness.

Acts 20:19   I served the Lord with all humility and with the tears and trials that came to me.

Rom. 12:11   Do not grow slack in zeal, be fervent in spirit, serve the Lord.

Rom. 14:17-18   For the kingdom of God is not a matter of food and drink, but of righteousness, peace, and joy in the holy Spirit; whoever serves Christ in this way is pleasing to God and approved by others.

1Pet. 4:10   As each one has received a gift, use it to serve one another as good stewards of God's varied grace.

SOUL

Each of us has a soul,
but we forget to value it.
We don't remember that
we are creatures made
in the image of God.
We don't understand the
great secrets hidden inside of us.

St. Teresa of Avila

Soul

Soul was a word I heard of many times as a child growing up in Catholic school. I remember the day that the priest who came in asked the group, "Where is your soul?" What an elusive thing our soul is! To try to find a concrete explanation, well I am still seeking it.

When I think of soul, the words deep, authentic, and sacred come to mind. To contemplate my soul, I seem to have to go beyond my usual way of reasoning and truly ... GO DEEP! Deep where words cannot describe or explain, but my spirit seems to resonate with this precious place.

It helped me to imagine my soul as a "secret garden" that only God and I can enter. My slow deep breathing in prayer would help me to go down deep into myself where the garden dwells. There I had created a safe place to simply be with God. My favorite wooden bench was our meeting place underneath a flowering cherry tree. There I would wait for God. Sometimes God was already there.

Deep, slow breaths can open the gateway into my soul and I can go there anytime, anyplace. I am so grateful to the spiritual guides I have had during my faith journey. These special guides have helped me discover the depth and beauty of my soul. It is as if we need someone to hold up a mirror that we may see ourselves more clearly. May you discover great light and joy in your soul, when you too go searching!

Reflection Questions:

How do you image your soul?

Is your soul more like....

... an overgrown jungle with thick underbrush ...
... a well tended garden ...
... a scenic overlook of wonder ...
... ? ...

Soul

Deut. 4:29   Yet there too you shall seek the Lord, your God; and you shall indeed find him when you search after him with your whole heart and your whole soul.

Deut. 6:5   Therefore, you shall love the Lord, your God, with all your heart, and with all your soul, and with all your strength.

Deut. 30:6   The Lord, your God, will circumcise your hearts and the hearts of your descendants, that you may love the Lord, your God, with all your heart and all your soul, and so may live.

1Chr. 22:19   Therefore, devote your hearts and souls to seeking the Lord your God.

1Chr. 28:9   As for you, … know the God of your father and serve him with a perfect heart and a willing soul, for the Lord searches all hearts and understands all the mind's thoughts. If you seek him, he will let himself be found by you.

Job 33:28   He delivered my soul from passing to the pit, /and I behold the light of life.

Ps. 13:3   How long must I carry sorrow in my soul, /grief in my heart day after day? / How long will my enemy triumph over me?

Ps. 16:9   Therefore my heart is glad, my soul rejoices; / my body also dwells secure.

Ps. 19:8   The law of the Lord is perfect, /refreshing the soul.

Ps. 25:1	I wait for you, O LORD; / I lift up my soul to my God.
Ps. 33:20	Our soul waits for the LORD, / who is our help and shield.
Ps. 34:3	My soul will glory in the LORD / that the poor may hear and be glad.
Ps. 42:2	As the deer longs for streams of water, /so my soul longs for you, O God.
Ps. 42:5	Those times I recall /as I pour out my soul.
Ps. 42:7	My soul is downcast within me; / therefore I will remember you.
Ps. 42:12	Why are you downcast, my soul, / why do you groan within me? / Wait for God, whom I shall praise again, / my savior and my God.
Ps. 57:9	Awake, my soul; /awake, lyre and harp! / I will wake the dawn!
Ps. 62:2	My soul rests in God alone, / from whom comes my salvation.
Ps. 62:6	My soul, be at rest in God alone, / from whom comes my hope.
Ps. 63:2	O God, you are my God — / for you I long! / For you my body yearns; / for you my soul thirsts.
Ps. 63:6	My soul shall savor the rich banquet of praise, / with joyous lips my mouth shall honor you!
Ps. 63:9	My soul clings fast to you; / your right hand upholds me.

Ps. 84:3   My soul yearns and pines for the courts of the Lord. My heart and flesh cry out for the living God.

Ps. 86:4   Gladden the soul of your servant; / to you, Lord, I lift up my soul.

Ps. 103:1   Bless the LORD, my soul; / all my being, bless his holy name!

Ps. 103:2   Bless the LORD, my soul; / do not forget all the gifts of God!

Ps. 104:1   Bless the LORD, my soul! / LORD, my God, you are great indeed!

Ps. 116:8-9   For my soul has been freed from death, / my eyes from tears, my feet from stumbling. / I shall walk before the Lord / in the land of the living.

Ps. 119:81   My soul longs for your salvation; / I put my hope in your word.

Ps. 130:5   I wait with longing for the LORD, / my soul waits for his word.

Ps. 131:2   Rather, I have stilled my soul, / hushed it like a weaned child. / Like a weaned child on its mother's lap, / so is my soul within me.

Ps. 146:2   Praise the LORD, my soul; / I shall praise the LORD all my life, / sing praise to my God while I live.

Pro. 2:10   For wisdom will enter your heart, / knowledge will please your soul.

Wis. 3:1   But the souls of the just are in the hand of God, / and no torment shall touch them.

Wis. 7:27-28　And passing into holy souls from age to age, / she produces friends of God and prophets. / For there is nought God loves, / be it not one who dwells with Wisdom.

Wis. 11:26　But you spare all things, because they are yours, O LORD and lover of souls.

Sir. 6:27　(of wisdom) With all your soul draw close to her; / with all your strength keep her ways.

Is. 26:9　My soul yearns for you in the night, / yes, my spirit within me keeps vigil for you.

Is. 61:10　I rejoice heartily in the LORD, / in my God is the joy of my soul.

Jer. 32:41　I will take delight in doing good to them: I will replant them firmly in this land, with all my heart and soul.

Lam. 3:24　My portion is the LORD, says my soul; / therefore will I hope in him.

Matt. 26:38　"My soul is sorrowful even to death. Remain here and keep watch with me."

Mk. 12:30　You shall love the Lord your God with all your heart, with all your soul, with all your mind, and with all your strength.

Lk. 1:46　"My soul proclaims the greatness of the Lord!"

Acts 2:26-27　Therefore my heart has been glad and my tongue has exulted; / my flesh, too, will dwell in hope, / because you will not abandon my soul to the nether world, / nor will you suffer your holy one to see corruption.

1Thes. 5:23   May the God of peace himself make you perfectly holy and may you entirely, spirit, soul, and body, be preserved blameless for the coming of our Lord Jesus Christ.

Heb. 4:12   Indeed, the word of God is living and effective, sharper than any two-edged sword, penetrating even between soul and spirit, joints and marrow, and able to discern reflections and thoughts of the heart.

Ja. 5:20   He should know that whoever brings back a sinner from the error of his way will save his soul from death and will cover a multitude of sins.

1Pe. 2:11   Beloved, I urge you as aliens and sojourners to keep away from worldly desires that wage war against the soul.

3Jn. 2   Beloved, I hope you are prospering in every respect and are in good health, just as your soul is prospering.

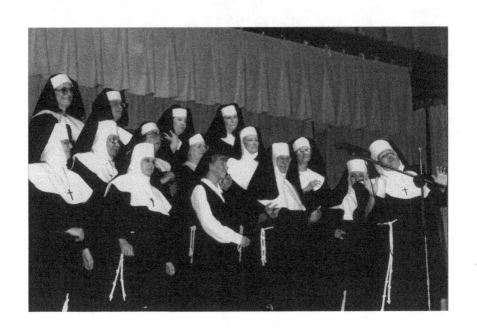

SPIRIT

A glad spirit
attains to perfection
more quickly
than any other.

St. Phillip Neri

Spirit

Spirit, the essence of our inner selves, inner strength, and the third person of the Holy Spirit that dwells within each of us. What a powerful word spirit is to reflect upon!

I may be flesh and bones, but I am also empowered with a spirit that is deeper than flesh. God breathed on me and filled me with God's spirit, the essence of my true self. It is this spirit that gets me through the tough times. When my spirit is struggling, God's spirit restores me.

Whenever I experience afflictive emotions, (those emotions that really get under your skin), I ask myself, "Is this my spirit talking, or my ego?" Throughout my life, I let my EGO have too much influence in all matters. That was not good, for my ego brought me much suffering. Rather, if I can sense where my spirit is guiding me, I find more harmony!

As for the third person of the Blessed Trinity ...

I see God the Father as Creator, the one who created me with love and desire.

I see Jesus as the One who loved me so much that He gave His life for me and calls me Friend.

I see the Spirit as my Dance Teacher. I believe that I am not just to walk this path of discipleship ... I am to dance with a true abandon!

Until God's spirit and I are one ...
well that's the goal!

Reflection Questions:

What shape is your spirit in right now?
Up and ready?
Need a shot of adrenalin?
Call EMS? (Emergency Master Spirit)
How do you define, describe the Holy Spirit in your life?

SPIRIT

2Sam. 23:2   The spirit of the LORD spoke through me; / his word was on my tongue.

Judith 16:14   You sent forth your spirit, and they were created; / no one can resist your word.

Job 10:12   Grace and favor you granted me, / and your providence has preserved my spirit.

Job 32:8   But it is a spirit in man, / the breath of the Almighty, that gives him understanding.

Ps. 31:6   Into your hands I commend my spirit; / you will redeem me, LORD, faithful God.

Ps. 51:12   A clean heart create for me, God; / renew in me a steadfast spirit.

Ps. 51:14   Restore my joy in your salvation; / sustain in me a willing spirit.

Ps. 138:3   When I cried out, you answered; / you strengthened my spirit.

Ps. 139:7   Where can I hide from your spirit? / From your presence, where can I flee?

Pro. 1:23   Lo! I will pour out to you my spirit, / I will acquaint you with my words.

Pro. 29:23   Man's pride causes his humiliation, / but he who is humble of spirit obtains honor.

Is. 11:2	The spirit of the LORD shall rest upon him; / a spirit of wisdom and of understanding, / A spirit of counsel and of strength, / a spirit of knowledge and of fear of the Lord.
Is. 26:9	My soul yearns for you in the night, / yes, my spirit within me keeps vigil for you.
Is. 42:1	Here is my servant whom I uphold, / my chosen one with whom I am pleased. / Upon whom I have put my spirit.
Is. 44:3	I will pour out water upon the thirsty ground, /and streams upon the dry land; / I will pour out my spirit upon your offspring, /and my blessing upon your descendants.
Is. 57:15	On high I dwell, and in holiness, / and with crushed and dejected in spirit, / To revive the hearts of the crushed.
Is. 61:1	The spirit of the Lord GOD is upon me, / because the LORD has anointed me; / He has sent me to bring glad tidings to the lowly, / to heal the brokenhearted, / To proclaim liberty to the captives / and release to the prisoners.
Ez. 36:26	I will give you a new heart and place a new spirit within you, taking from your bodies your stony hearts and giving you natural hearts.
Ez. 37:14	I will put my spirit in you that you may live, and I will settle you upon your land; thus you shall know that I am the Lord. I have promised, and I will do it, says the Lord.

Dan. 5:14 I have heard that the spirit of God is in you, that you possess brilliant knowledge and extraordinary wisdom.

Joel 3:1 Then afterward I will pour out / my spirit upon all mankind. / Your sons and daughters shall prophesy, / your old men shall dream dreams, / your young men shall see visions.

Zech. 4:6 Not by an army, nor by might, but by my spirit, says the LORD of hosts.

Mt. 3:16 After Jesus was baptized, he came up from the water and behold, the heavens were opened [for him], and he saw the Spirit of God descending like a dove [and] coming upon him.

Mt. 5:3 Blessed are the poor in spirit, / for theirs is the kingdom of heaven.

Mt. 10:19-20 When they hand you over, do not worry about how you are to speak or what you are to say. You will be given at that moment what you are to say. For it will not be you who speak but the Spirit of your Father speaking through you.

Mt. 12:18 Behold, my servant whom I have chosen, / my beloved in whom I delight; / I shall place my spirit upon him, / and he will proclaim justice to the Gentiles.

Mt. 26:41 Watch and pray that you may not undergo the test. The spirit is willing, but the flesh is weak.

Mt. 28:19 Go, therefore, and make disciples of all nations, baptizing them in the name of the Father, and of the Son, and of the holy Spirit.

Lk. 1:46-47   My soul proclaims the greatness of the Lord; / my spirit rejoices in God my savior.

Lk. 4:18-19   The Spirit of the Lord is upon me, / because he has anointed me / to bring glad tidings to the poor. / He has sent me to proclaim liberty to captives / and recovery of sight to the blind, / to let the oppressed go free, / and to proclaim a year acceptable to the Lord.

Lk. 23:46   "Father, into your hands I commend my spirit."

Jn. 3:5   Amen, amen, I say to you, no one can enter the kingdom of God without being born of water and Spirit.

Jn. 4:23   But the hour is coming, and is now here, when true worshipers will worship the Father in Spirit and truth; and indeed the Father seeks such people to worship him.

Jn. 4:24   God is Spirit, and those who worship him must worship in Spirit and truth.

Jn. 7:38-39   Whoever believes in me, as scripture says, / "Rivers of living water will flow from within him."/ He said this in reference to the Spirit that those who came to believe in him were to receive.

Jn. 14:16-17   And I will ask the Father, and he will give you another Advocate to be with you always, the Spirit of truth, which the world cannot accept, because it neither sees nor knows it. But you know it, because it remains with you, and will be in you.

Jn. 14:26   The Advocate, the holy Spirit that the Father will send in my name— he will teach you everything and remind you of all that I told you.

Jn. 16:13   But when he comes, the Spirit of truth, he will guide you to all truth.

Jn. 20:22   And when he had said this, he breathed on them and said to them, "Receive the holy Spirit."

Acts 2:4   And they were all filled with the holy Spirit and began to speak in different tongues, as the Spirit enabled them to proclaim.

Acts 2:38   Repent and be baptized, every one of you, in the name of Jesus Christ for the forgiveness of your sins; and you will receive the gift of the holy Spirit.

Acts 7:59   Lord Jesus, receive my spirit.

Rom. 8:9   But you are not in the flesh; on the contrary, you are in the spirit, if only the Spirit of God dwells in you.

Rom. 8:14   For those who are led by the Spirit of God are children of God.

Rom. 8:15   For you did not receive a spirit of slavery to fall back into fear, but you received a spirit of adoption, through which we cry, "*Abba*, Father!"

Rom. 8:26   In the same way, the Spirit too comes to the aid of our weakness; for we do not know how to pray as we ought, but the Spirit itself intercedes with inexpressible groanings.

Rom. 15:13   May the God of hope fill you with all joy and peace in believing, so that you may abound in hope by the power of the holy Spirit.

1Cor. 3:16   Do you not know that you are the temple of God, and that the Spirit of God dwells in you?

1Cor. 12:7	To each individual the manifestation of the Spirit is given for some benefit.
2Cor. 3:2-3	You are our letter, written on our hearts, known and read by all, shown to be a letter of Christ administered by us, written not in ink but by the Spirit of the living God, not on tablets of stone but on tablets that are hearts of flesh.
2Cor. 3:17	Now the Lord is the Spirit, and where the Spirit of the Lord is, there is freedom.
2Cor. 3:18	All of us gazing with unveiled face on the glory of the Lord, are being transformed into the same image from glory to glory, as from the Lord who is the Spirit.
Gal. 4:6-7	As proof that you are children, God sent the spirit of his Son into our hearts, crying out, "Abba, Father!" So you are no longer a slave but a child, and if a child then also an heir, through God.
Gal. 5:5	For through the Spirit, by faith, we await the hope of righteousness.
Gal. 5:22-23	The fruit of the Spirit is love, joy, peace, patience, kindness, generosity, faithfulness, gentleness, self-control.
Eph. 2:22	In him you also are being built together into a dwelling place of God in the Spirit.
Eph. 3:16	… that he may grant you in accord with the riches of his glory to be strengthened with power through his Spirit in the inner self.
Eph. 4:4	One body and one Spirit, as you were also called to the one hope of your call.

Eph. 4:23-24 And be renewed in the spirit of your minds, and put on the new self, created in God's way in righteousness and holiness of truth.

Eph. 6:17 … And take the helmet of salvation and the sword of the Spirit, which is the word of God.

Phil. 2:1-2 If there is any encouragement in Christ, any solace in love, any participation in the Spirit, any compassion and mercy, complete my joy by being of the same mind, with the same love, united in heart, thinking one thing.

1Thes. 5:23 May the God of peace himself make you perfectly holy and may you entirely, spirit, soul, and body, be preserved blameless for the coming of our Lord Jesus Christ.

2Tim. 1:7 For God did not give us a spirit of cowardice but rather of power and love and self-control.

Heb. 4:12 Indeed, the word of God is living and effective, sharper than any two-edged sword, penetrating even between soul and spirit, joints and marrow, and able to discern reflections and thoughts of the heart.

1Pet. 4:14 If you are insulted for the name of Christ, blessed are you, for the Spirit of glory and of God rests upon you.

Jude 20 Beloved, build yourselves up in your most holy faith; pray in the holy Spirit.

Rev. 22:17 The Spirit and the bride say, "Come." Let the hearer say, "Come." Let the one who thirsts come forward, and the one who wants it receive the gift of life-giving water.

STRENGTH

Nothing is so strong
as gentleness,
nothing is so gentle
as real strength.

St. Francis De Sales

STRENGTH

To think of strength, a strong man comes to mind. It seems that all men possess the strength to lift items that I struggle to lift. God just empowered men with this ability of physical strength. However, it has been said that if a man gave birth, we probably would have fewer children. Women's strength is shown in their ability to persevere in childbirth, to multitask in a normal family day and yet to be that strength for others when it is needed. Then I look at the children in our world who find the strength to come through their parents divorces, illnesses, peer pressure, and bullying. What of spiritual strength? Who are the ones we turn to and say, "Please pray for me?"

Strength is a word that seems to give hope and encouragement. This precious gift can help us get through and conquer whatever problem may be before us. People are looking for strength to face and fight their cancer; addictions, prejudice and hate. Perhaps many simply want the strength to get out of bed in the morning when their depression wants to hold them down. There are those looking for the strength to forgive the ones who have truly hurt them. Spiritual strength is needed to fight off temptation and sin.

How do I see strength? I imagine strength as a strong oak tree. This precious symbol teaches me that strength comes from:

Staying rooted in the earth ...
Keeping the roots connected to life-giving water ...
Stretching those branches to receive the light ...
Having wisdom to bend with the storms of life.

My husband, who is so in tune with nature, reminds me that a trees' roots grow best through the long, dark winter months. Adversity can strengthen all! So there is goodness in all the storms in our life! Strength will come to me if I stay rooted in God, the faith community, and prayer. Letting wisdom encourage me to bend with the storms of life, I will not break; but be strengthened!

My greatest place to find strength is in Scripture ... even in the individual words. Whenever I am in need, I ask God, "What word would you give me today?" The needed word is always given! Strength is closer than we think!

Reflection Questions:

Where do you draw your strength?

Who draws strength from /through you?

STRENGTH

Ex. 15:2 My strength and my courage is the LORD, / and he has been my savior.

1Chr. 16:11 Look to the LORD in his strength; / seek to serve him constantly.

Neh. 8:10 Rejoicing in the LORD must be your strength.

Ps. 18:2 I love you, LORD, my strength.

Ps. 23:1-3 The LORD is my shepherd; / there is nothing I lack. / In green pastures you let me graze; / to safe waters you lead me; / you restore my strength.

Ps. 28:7 The LORD is my strength and my shield, / in whom my heart trusted and found help. / So my heart rejoices; / with my song I praise my God.

Ps. 46:2 God is our refuge and our strength, / an ever-present help in distress.

Ps. 59:10-11 My strength, for you I watch; / you, God, are my fortress, my loving God.

Ps. 59:17 But I shall sing of your strength, / extol your love at dawn.

Ps. 59:18 My strength, your praise I will sing; / you, God, are my fortress, my loving God.

Ps. 61:4-5 You are my refuge, / a tower of strength against the foe. / Then I will ever dwell in your tent, / take refuge in the shelter of your wings.

Ps. 71:6	On you I depend since birth; / from my mother's womb you are my strength; / my hope in you never wavers.
Ps. 92:11	You have given me the strength of a wild bull; / you have poured rich oil upon me.
Ps. 119:116-117	Sustain me by your promise that I may live; / do not disappoint me in my hope. / Strengthen me that I may be safe.
Ps. 138:1, 3	I thank you, LORD, with all my heart. / When I cried out, you answered; / you strengthened my spirit.
Pro. 31:25	She is clothed with strength and dignity, / and she laughs at the days to come.
Sir. 6:27	With all your soul draw close to her; / with all your strength keep her ways. (concerning wisdom)
Is. 11:2	The spirit of the LORD shall rest upon him: / a spirit of wisdom and of understanding, / A spirit of counsel and of strength, / a spirit of knowledge and of fear of the Lord.
Is. 12:2	God indeed is my savior; / I am confident and un-afraid. / My strength and my courage is the Lord, / and he has been my savior.
Is. 30:15	For thus says the Lord GOD, / the Holy One of Israel: / By waiting and by calm you shall be saved, / in quiet and in trust your strength lies.
Is. 33:2	O LORD, have pity on us, for you we wait. / Be our strength every morning, / our salvation in time of trouble!

Is. 40:31   They that hope in the Lord will renew their strength, / they will soar as with eagles' wings; / They will run and not grow weary, / walk and not grow faint.

Is. 41:10   Fear not, I am with you; / be not dismayed; I am your God. / I will strengthen you, and help you, / and uphold you with my right hand of justice.

Is. 58:11   The Lord will guide you always / and give you plenty even on the parched land. / He will renew your strength, / and you shall be like a watered garden, / like a spring whose water never fails.

Dan. 10:18-19   The one who looked like a man touched me again and strengthened me, saying, "Fear not, beloved, you are safe; take courage and be strong."

Dan. 10:20   When he spoke to me, I grew strong and said, "Speak, my lord, for you have strengthened me."

Hab. 3:19   God, my Lord, is my strength; / he makes my feet swift as those of hinds / and enables me to go upon the heights.

Zech. 10:12   I will strengthen them in the Lord, / and they shall walk in his name, says the Lord.

Mk. 12:30   You shall love the Lord your God with all your heart, with all your soul, with all your mind, and with all your strength.

Lk. 10:27   You shall love the Lord, your God, with all your heart, with all your being, with all your strength, and with all your mind, and your neighbor as yourself.

Lk. 22:42-43   "Father, if you are willing, take this cup away from me; still, not my will but yours be done." [And to strengthen him, an angel from heaven appeared to him.]

1Cor. 10:13   No trial has come to you but what is human. God is faithful and will not let you be tried beyond your strength; but with the trial he will also provide a way out, so that you may be able to bear it.

2Cor. 12:8, 10   My grace is sufficient for you, for power is made perfect in weakness. Therefore, I am content with weaknesses, insults, hardships, persecutions, and constraints, for the sake of Christ; for when I am weak, then I am strong.

Eph. 3:14, 16   For this reason I kneel before the Father, ... that he may grant you in accord with the riches of his glory to be strengthened with power through his Spirit in the inner self.

Eph. 3:17-19   That Christ may dwell in your hearts through faith; that you, rooted and grounded in love, may have strength to comprehend with all the holy ones what is the breadth and length and height and depth and to know the love of Christ that surpasses knowledge, so that you may be filled with all the fullness of God.

Eph. 6:10 -11   Draw your strength from the Lord and from his mighty power. Put on the armor of God so that you may be able to stand firm against the tactics of the devil.

Phil. 4:13   I have the strength for everything through him who empowers me.

1Thes. 3:12-13   May the Lord make you increase and abound in love for one another and for all, just as we have for you, so as to strengthen your hearts to be blameless in holiness before our God.

2Thes. 2:16-17 May our Lord Jesus Christ himself and God our Father, who has loved us and given us everlasting encouragement and good hope through his grace, encourage your hearts and strengthen them in every good deed and word.

2Thes. 3:3 The Lord is faithful; he will strengthen you and guard you from the evil one.

1Tim. 1:12 I am grateful to him who has strengthened me, Christ Jesus our Lord, because he considered me trustworthy in appointing me to the ministry.

Heb. 13:9 It is good to have our hearts strengthened by grace.

1Pet. 5:10 The God of all grace who called you to his eternal glory through Christ [Jesus] will himself restore, confirm, strengthen, and establish you after you have suffered a little.

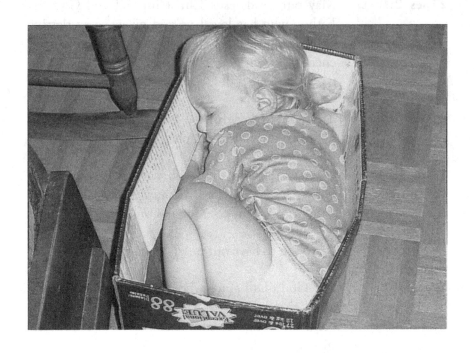

TRUST

If we really belong to God,
then we must trust in God.
We must never be
preoccupied with the future.
There is no reason to be,
God is there.

Mother Teresa

TRUST

"In God we Trust," really? In the last year, leaving these words on our money has become a real issue. Let us look at it from a different view ... Do we really trust in God? Even with money, we trust God as long as it is insured by the National Bank Reserve. Do we not make sure that our banks are federally insured? Of course, there are the insurances for life, death, floods, vacations and cars! If we really trusted God then why do so many doubt that marriage can last a lifetime? If we trusted, then why are so many of us, "control freaks"?

I find this within myself. Even when I pray, I have a habit of telling God what I think will work! When do I trust that God sees the bigger picture and knows what is best? Trust takes a lot of work. First of all, I need to see myself in a humble light ... God is God and I am not! I do not have all the answers.

Trust is difficult for me, ask any salesperson, I am very skeptical! How many times in my life have I been let down or even dropped by friends and family and yes, even church ... lots! Praying with the scripture stories, I discovered that Jesus too had the problem of friends who let him down. Jesus never gave up on them. He simply loved and in loving comes a lot of forgiving! Perhaps, I just needed the reminder that people are human, not perfect. I am learning to trust that even if things don't go as I want, or if people let me down ... it will be okay!

What would happen if we lived in trust? Would we discover a life free of anxiety, fears and tension? Would we find peace? After all, no matter what happens, our God can bring great goodness out of chaos. Just trust!

Patti King

Reflection Questions:

How are you about trusting?

If you were asked to close your eyes & fall backwards for:
... a group of people to catch you?
... God?

1. Would you fall freely, totally trusting them?
2. Would you demand a bunch of pillows ... just in case?
3. Would you try ...but decide, I don't think so?
4. Would you already have left the room?

What needs to change in you that you may trust?

TRUST

Ps. 9:11	Those who honor your name trust in you; / you never forsake those who seek you, Lord.
Ps. 13:6	I trust in your faithfulness, / grant my heart joy in your help, / That I may sing of the Lord, "How good our God has been to me!"
Ps. 18:31	God's way is unerring; / the LORD's promise is tried and true; / he is a shield for all who trust in him.
Ps. 25:1	I wait for you, O LORD; I lift up my soul to my God. / In you I trust; do not let me be disgraced.
Ps. 25:20	Preserve my life and rescue me; / do not let me be disgraced, for I trust in you.
Ps. 26:1	Grant me justice, LORD! / I have walked without blame. / In the LORD I have trusted; / I have not faltered.
Ps. 27:3	Though an army encamp against me, / my heart does not fear; / Though war be waged against me, / even then do I trust.
Ps. 28:7	The LORD is my strength and my shield, / in whom my heart trusted and found help.
Ps. 31:7-8	I trust in the LORD. / I will rejoice and be glad in your love.
Ps. 31:15	I trust in you, LORD; / I say, "You are my God."
Ps. 32:10	Love surrounds those who trust in the LORD.

Ps. 33:4   For the Lord's word is true; / all his works are trustworthy.

Ps. 33:21   For in God our hearts rejoice; / in your holy name we trust.

Ps. 37:3   Trust in the Lord and do good / that you may dwell in the land and live secure.

Ps. 37:5   Commit your way to the Lord; / trust that God will act.

Ps. 52:10   But, I, like an olive tree in the house of God, / trust in God's faithful love forever.

Ps. 56:3-4   O Most High, when I am afraid, / in you I place my trust.

Ps. 71:5   You are my hope, Lord; / my trust, God, from my youth.

Ps. 84:13   O Lord of hosts, / happy are those who trust in you!

Ps. 85:9   I will listen for the word of God; / surely the Lord will proclaim peace / To his people, to the faithful, / to those who trust in him.

Ps. 91:2   "My refuge and fortress, / my God in whom I trust."

Ps. 119:66   Teach me wisdom and knowledge, / for in your commands I trust.

Ps. 125:1   Like Mount Zion are they / who trust in the Lord, / unshakeable, forever enduring.

Ps. 143:8   At dawn let me hear of your kindness, / for in you I trust. / Show me the path I should walk, / for to you I entrust my life.

Ps. 144:2	My safeguard and my fortress, / my stronghold, my deliverer, / My shield, in whom I trust.
Ps. 145:13	The LORD is trustworthy in every word, / and faithful in every work.
Pro. 3:5	Trust in the LORD with all your heart, / on your own intelligence rely not.
Pro. 16:20	Happy is he who trusts in the LORD!
Pro. 28:25	He who trusts in the LORD will prosper.
Pro. 29:25	He who trusts in the LORD is safe.
Wis. 3:9	Those who trust in him shall understand truth, / and the faithful shall abide with him in love.
Sir. 2:6	Trust God and he will help you; / make straight your ways and hope in him.
Sir. 11:21	Trust in the LORD and wait for his light.
Is. 8:17	For I will trust in the LORD; ... yes, I will wait for him.
Is. 26:4	Trust in the LORD forever! / For the LORD is an eternal Rock.
Is. 30:15	For thus says the Lord GOD, / the Holy One of Israel: / By waiting and by calm you shall be saved, / in quiet and in trust your strength lies.
Jer. 17:7	Blessed is the man who trusts in the LORD, / whose hope is the LORD.
1Tim. 6:20	Guard what has been entrusted to you.

2Tim. 1:14   Guard this rich trust with the help of the holy Spirit that dwells within us.

Heb. 10:23   Let us hold unwaveringly to our confession that gives us hope, for he who made the promise is trustworthy.

TRUTH

O my God, I really want to listen to You;
I beg You to answer me when I say humbly:
What is truth?
Make me see things as they really are.
Let nothing cause me to be deceived.

Therese of Lisieux

TRUTH

Truth is elusive. Even a married couple of 30 years, may give "their version" of a story and it may be nothing alike! As a Mom, I have heard so many times, "I didn't do it," with fingers pointing to someone else. We have learned to live with mysteries at our house, since we cannot find the truth about those "unsolved cases" of who did it!

Even through the internet we have to question the truthfulness of what we have received. On receiving an email with passed on information, I try to check it out for it's validity before passing it on. A precious gentleman very generously gave me a site to seek out truth, snopes.com. Most of the time when I look up the information, I find that it is false. I even checked out an email that said it had been checked by snopes.com ... again, it was false! How many people received this email and passed it on to another group ... and another? Although we would like to think of ourselves as truthful, how many times have we passed on untruths through the email or gossip? How can one come to truth? It is not as easy as we would like.

Most of the time I have to simply trust in the mystery of the moment, knowing that in time, truth will reveal itself. Time, patient waiting and being alert has brought me the answers I need. I realize that each person sees the truth through their own "lenses of lived experience." We may never quite agree on what is truth. I lean on the knowledge that Jesus revealed to us when he said,

I am the way and the truth and the life.
Jn.14:6

The only real truth that I can be sure of is JESUS. I often say:

If Jesus is the truth, then I do not need to fear truth.
Whatever it is, it will be okay, ... for Jesus is in the midst!

Patti King

This has brought me courage during tough times, especially when the truth is about the real me. It is very hard to face the truth about my faults and failings. It seems that when it comes to seeing the truth about ourselves, we would rather keep our eyes closed!

Reflection Questions:

Letting God guide you in prayer, look at yourself in truth.

What do you see?
What does God see? Ask God.
How can you learn to "live in truth"

TRUTH

Tobit 3:2   You are righteous, O Lord, / and all your deeds are just; / All your ways are mercy and truth.

Ps. 15:1-2   LORD, who may abide in your tent? / Who may dwell on your holy mountain? / Whoever walks without blame, / doing what is right, / speaking truth from the heart.

Ps. 25:5   Guide me in your truth and teach me, / for you are God my savior, / For you I wait all the long day, / because of your goodness, Lord.

Ps. 85:11   Love and truth will meet; / justice and peace will kiss.

Ps. 85:12   Truth will spring up from the earth; / justice will look down from heaven.

Ps. 86:11   Teach me, LORD, your way / that I may walk in your truth, / single-hearted and revering your name.

Ps. 119:43   Do not take the word of truth from my mouth, / for in your edicts is my hope.

Ps. 145:18   You, LORD, are near to all who call upon you, / to all who call upon you in truth.

Wis. 3:9   Those who trust in him shall understand truth, / and the faithful shall abide with him in love: / Because grace and mercy are with his holy ones.

Sir. 37:15   Most important of all, pray to God / to set your feet in the path of truth.

Jer. 23:28 Let the prophet who has a dream recount his dream; let him who has my word speak my word truthfully!

Zech. 8:16 These then are the things you should do: Speak the truth to one another; let there be honesty and peace in the judgments at your gates.

Jn. 1:14 And the Word became flesh /and made his dwelling among us, / and we saw his glory, / the glory as of the Father's only Son, / full of grace and truth.

Jn. 3:21 But whoever lives the truth comes to the light, so that his works may be clearly seen as done in God.

Jn. 4:23 But the hour is coming, and is now here, when true worshippers will worship the Father in Spirit and truth; and indeed the Father seeks such people to worship him.

Jn. 4:24 God is Spirit, and those who worship him must worship in Spirit and truth.

Jn. 8:31-32 If you remain in my word, you will truly be my disciples, and you will know the truth, and the truth will set you free.

Jn. 14:6 Jesus said, "I am the way and the truth and the life."

Jn. 14:17 The Spirit of truth, which the world cannot accept, because it neither sees nor knows it. But you know it, because it remains with you.

Jn. 15:26 When the Advocate comes whom I will send you from the Father, the Spirit of truth that proceeds from the Father, he will testify to me.

Jn. 16:13 But when he comes, the Spirit of truth, he will guide you to all truth.

Jn. 17:17	Consecrate them in the truth. Your word is truth.
Jn. 17:19	I consecrate myself for them, so that they also may be consecrated in truth.
Jn. 18:37	For this I was born and for this I came into the world, to testify to the truth. Everyone who belongs to the truth, listens to my voice.
Rom. 9:1	I speak the truth in Christ, I do not lie.
1Cor. 13:4, 6	Love is patient. ... It does not rejoice over wrongdoing but rejoices with the truth.
Eph. 1:13	In him you also, who have heard the word of truth, the gospel of your salvation, and have believed in him, were sealed with the promised holy Spirit.
Eph. 4:15	Rather, living the truth in love, we should grow in every way into him who is the head, Christ.
Eph. 4:23-24	Be renewed in the spirit of your minds, and put on the new self, created in God's way in righteousness and holiness of truth.
Eph. 5:8-9	You are light in the Lord. Live as children of light, for light produces every kind of goodness and righteousness and truth.
Eph. 6:14-15	So stand fast with your loins girded in truth, clothed with righteousness as a breastplate, and your feet shod in readiness for the gospel of peace.

Phil. 4:8	Whatever is true, whatever is honorable, whatever is just, whatever is pure, whatever is lovely, whatever is gracious, if there is any excellence and if there is anything worthy of praise, think about these things.
2Tim. 2:15	Be eager to present yourselves as acceptable to God, a workman who causes no disgrace, imparting the word of truth without deviation.
1Pet. 1:22	Since you have purified yourselves by obedience to the truth for sincere mutual love, love one another intensely from a [pure] heart.
1Jn. 3:18	Children, let us love not in word or speech but in deed and truth.
3Jn. 3	I rejoiced greatly when some of the brothers came and testified to how truly you walk in the truth.
3Jn. 4	Nothing gives me greater joy than to hear that my children are walking in the truth.

WISDOM

The invariable mark of wisdom
is to see the miraculous
in the common.

Ralph Waldo Emerson

WISDOM

Wisdom to me, is more than knowledge and more than understanding. I know many people who have many college degrees but seem to have no wisdom. Then there is the peasant woman who has no formal education, but is so very filled with wisdom.

Wisdom is a deeper gift that comes from God. Like a beacon of light that shines through the darkness, wisdom fills us with that "deeper knowing" to guide us. One of my favorite scripture stories in grade school was the story of Solomon, who asked for wisdom to lead his people. I was always moved that this man would choose wisdom over riches and honor. It touched my heart so much, that I too began to pray for wisdom.

Who in my life do I see as a person of wisdom? This will probably be the person that I turn to when I am trying to discern an answer to one of life's questions. Usually, I find it in the person who has experienced life, like Grandma Wilks who went through the Great Depression. Then there is my Mom who still amazes me with her knowledge and intuition. Let us not overlook those who are younger, for I have had the wisest words come from my grandchildren! If I am looking for spiritual wisdom I turn to some very special mentors in my life. A precious pastor told us many times that we will do better, if we rely on the wisdom of the group, especially a group centered in prayer. I find this to be so true, especially within my Bible Study Group!

In our modern day world, what we need is … great wisdom! We need this gift in our world leaders, our church leaders and in ourselves. Let us open ourselves to the "wisdom of God," that this precious gift may mature within each of us. May wisdom become for us an eternal light that will guide us, no matter the darkness!

Reflection Questions:

How has God gifted you with wisdom?

What symbol would you use to describe wisdom in your life?

WISDOM

1Ki. 2:6	Act with the wisdom you possess.
1Ki. 10:8	Happy these servants of yours, who stand before you always and listen to your wisdom.
2Chr. 1:10	Give me, therefore, wisdom and knowledge to lead this people, for otherwise who could rule this great people of yours?
Ps. 19:8	The law of the LORD is perfect, / refreshing the soul. / The decree of the LORD is trustworthy, / giving wisdom to the simple.
Ps. 49:4	My mouth shall speak wisdom, / my heart shall offer insight.
Ps. 51:8	Still, you insist on sincerity of heart; / in my inmost being teach me wisdom.
Pro. 2:10	For wisdom will enter your heart, / knowledge will please your soul.
Pro. 3:13	Happy the man who finds wisdom, / the man who gains understanding!
Pro. 7:4	Say to Wisdom, "You are my sister!" / call Understanding, "Friend!"
Pro. 8:12	"I, Wisdom, dwell with experience, / and judicious knowledge I attain."
Pro. 9:10	The beginning of wisdom is the fear of the LORD, / and knowledge of the Holy One is understanding.

Pro. 14:33   In the heart of the intelligent wisdom abides.

Pro. 24:13-14   Virgin honey is sweet to your taste; / Such, you must know, is wisdom to your soul.

Pro. 31:26   She opens her mouth in wisdom, / and on her tongue is kindly counsel.

Wis. 6:12   Resplendent and unfading is Wisdom, / and she is readily perceived by those who love her, / and found by those who seek her.

Wis. 7:7   Therefore, I prayed, and prudence was given me; / I pleaded and the spirit of Wisdom came to me.

Wis. 7:24   For Wisdom is mobile beyond all motion, / and she penetrates and pervades all things by reason of her purity.

Wis. 7:27-28   And passing into holy souls from age to age, / she produces friends of God and prophets. / For there is nought God loves, be it not one who dwells with Wisdom.

Wis. 9:17   Who ever knew your counsel, except you had given Wisdom / and sent your holy spirit from on high?

Sir. 1:1   All wisdom comes from the LORD / and with him it remains forever.

Sir. 1:16   Wisdom's garland is fear of the LORD, / with blossoms of peace and perfect health.

Sir. 1:23   If you desire wisdom, keep the commandments, / and the LORD will bestow her upon you.

Sir. 4:23-24	Refrain not from speaking at the proper time, / and hide not away your wisdom; / For it is through speech that wisdom becomes known.
Sir. 6:37	Reflect on the precepts of the LORD, / let his commandments be your constant meditation; / Then he will enlighten your mind, / and the wisdom you desire he will grant.
Sir. 14:20	Happy the man who meditates on wisdom, / and reflects on knowledge.
Sir. 18:29	Those trained in her words must show their wisdom, / dispensing sound proverbs like life-giving waters.
Sir. 45:26	And now bless the LORD / who has crowned you with glory! / May he grant you wisdom of heart!
Is. 11:2	The spirit of the LORD shall rest upon him: / a spirit of wisdom and of understanding, / A spirit of counsel and of strength, / a spirit of knowledge and of fear of the Lord.
Dan. 2:23	To you, God of my fathers, / I give thanks and praise, / because you have given me wisdom and power.
Lk. 21:14-15	Remember, you are not to prepare your defense beforehand, for I myself shall give you a wisdom in speaking that all your adversaries will be powerless to resist or refute.
Rom. 11:33	Oh, the depth of the riches and wisdom and knowledge of God! How inscrutable are his judgments and how unsearchable his ways!

1Co. 2:6-7	Yet we do speak a wisdom to those who are mature, but not a wisdom of this age ... Rather we speak God's wisdom, mysterious, hidden, which God predetermined before the ages for our glory.
1Co. 2:13	And we speak about them not with words taught by human wisdom, but with words taught by the Spirit, describing spiritual realities in spiritual terms.
1Co. 12:4, 8	There are different kinds of spiritual gifts but the same Spirit. To one is given through the Spirit the expression of wisdom.
Eph. 1:16-17	Remembering you in my prayers, that the God of our Lord Jesus Christ, the Father of glory, may give you a spirit of wisdom and revelation resulting in knowledge of him.
Col. 1:9	Therefore, ... we do not cease praying for you and asking that you may be filled with the knowledge of his will through all spiritual wisdom and understanding.
Col. 2:2-3	... that their hearts may be encouraged as they are brought together in love, to have all the richness of fully assured understanding, for the knowledge of the mystery of God, Christ, in whom are hidden all the treasures of wisdom and knowledge.
Col. 3:16	Let the word of Christ dwell in you richly, as in all wisdom you teach and admonish one another, singing psalms, hymns, and spiritual songs with gratitude in your hearts to God.

2Tim. 3:15 …and that from infancy you have known [the] sacred scriptures, which are capable of giving you wisdom for salvation through faith in Christ Jesus.

Ja. 1:5 But if any of you lacks wisdom, he should ask God who gives to all generously and ungrudgingly, and he will be given it.

Ja. 3:13 Who among you is wise and understanding? Let him show his works by a good life in the humility that comes from wisdom.

Ja. 3:17 But the wisdom from above is first of all pure, then peaceable, gentle, compliant, full of mercy and good fruits, without inconstancy or insincerity.

WORD

O Lord, my God, how You possess
the words of eternal life,
where all mortals will find what they desire
if they want to seek it!

Teresa of Avila

WORD

In the beginning was the WORD,
and the WORD was with God,
and the WORD was God.
Jn. 1:1

One of the most important words we can reflect on is WORD, especially in the person of Jesus. The written WORD, the bible, takes on a life that can move, change and encourage all of us. Then there is the WORD that is spoken to be truly heard, as we hear it on Sundays at Church. As a lector, who proclaims the Word of God at the Sunday liturgy, I take this privilege very seriously. I pray with the scripture passage, study, and practice with the reading, until the passage is comfortable in my heart and on my lips.

Bible Study is one of my all time highlights during the week. To gather with a group of committed Christians and "break open the Word" is challenging, affirming and energizing! I encourage anyone whose heart is seeking the Word, to find a good bible study group and join it. Something very special happens when "two or three are gathered in Christ's name!"

Each "Word of God" has the power to help me see God, the faith community, and myself more clearly. God, the Master Sower, plants a word, like a seed deep in my soul. Over the next days, weeks, or months God waters and nurtures the word until such a day that the word blossoms up and bears fruit.

St. Francis of Assisi said to his brothers, "Go out and proclaim the gospel and only use words if you have to." You see, like Jesus, if the word truly dwells within me, then people should be able to see the word in me! If my word is Love, then it should radiate all over my face and in my touch.

Patti King

Reflection Questions:

How best does the WORD of God come to you ... written, verbal or in the person of Jesus?

Can people see you as a "reflection of the WORD"?

WORD

Ruth 2:13   May I prove worthy of your kindness, my lord: you have comforted me, your servant, with your consoling words; would indeed that I were a servant of yours!

2Sam. 7:28   Lord GOD, you are God and your words are truth.

Ps. 33:4   For the LORD's word is true; / all his works are trustworthy.

Ps. 85:9   I will listen for the word of God; / surely the LORD will proclaim peace / To his people, to the faithful, / to those who trust in him.

Ps. 119:17   Be kind to your servant that I may live, / that I may keep your word.

Ps. 119:49   Remember your word to your servant / by which you give me hope.

Ps. 119:57   My portion is the LORD; / I promise to keep your words.

Ps. 119:65   You have treated your servant well, / according to your word, O LORD.

Ps. 119:81   My soul longs for your salvation; / I put my hope in your word.

Ps. 119:105   Your word is a lamp for my feet, / a light for my path.

Ps. 119:114   You are my refuge and shield; / in your word I hope.

Ps. 119:130	The revelation of your words sheds light, / gives understanding to the simple.
Ps. 119:147	I rise before dawn and cry out; / I put my hope in your words.
Ps. 119:160	Your every word is enduring; / all your just edicts are forever.
Ps. 119:169	Let my cry come before you, LORD; / in keeping with your word give me discernment.
Ps. 130:5	I wait with longing for the LORD, / my soul waits for his word.
Ps. 140:7	I say to the LORD: You are my God; / listen, LORD, to the words of my prayer.
Ps. 145:13	The LORD is trustworthy in every word, / and faithful in every work.
Pro. 1:23	I will pour out to you my spirit, / I will acquaint you with my words.
Pro. 4:4	Let your heart hold fast my words; / keep my commands, that you may live!
Wis. 16:26	That your sons whom you loved might learn, O LORD, / that it is not the various kinds of fruits that nourish man, but it is your word that preserves those who believe you!
Sir. 33:4	Prepare your words and you will be listened to; / draw upon your training, and then give your answer.
Is. 50:4	The Lord GOD has given me / a well-trained tongue, / That I might know how to speak to the weary / a word that will rouse them.

Is. 55:10-11	For just as from the heavens / the rain and snow come down / And do not return there / till they have watered the earth, / making it fertile and fruitful, / Giving seed to him who sows / and bread to him who eats, / So shall my word be / that goes forth from my mouth; / It shall not return to me void, / but shall do my will, / achieving the end for which I sent it.
Jer. 15:16	When I found your words, I devoured them; / they became my joy and the happiness of my heart.
Jer. 20:8-9	The word of the LORD has brought me /derision and reproach all the day. / I say to myself, I will not mention him, / I will speak in his name no more. / But then it becomes like fire burning in my heart, / imprisoned in my bones; / I grow weary holding it in, / I cannot endure it.
Ez. 37:4-5	Then he said to me, Prophesy over these bones and say to them: Dry bones, hear the word of the Lord! Thus says the Lord God to these bones: See! I will bring spirit into you, that you may come to life!
Dan. 10:11	Daniel, beloved, ... understand the words which I am speaking to you; stand up, for my mission now is to you.
Matt. 4:4	One does not live by bread alone, / but by every word that comes forth from the mouth of God.
Matt. 6:7-8	In praying, do not babble like the pagans, who think that they will be heard because of their many words. Do not be like them. Your Father knows what you need before you ask him.
Matt. 8:8	Lord, I am not worthy to have you enter under my roof; only say the word and my servant will be healed.

Matt. 13:23 The seed sown on rich soil is the one who hears the word and understands it, who indeed bears fruit and yields a hundred or sixty or thirtyfold.

Matt. 24:35 Heaven and earth will pass away, but my words will not pass away.

Lk. 1:38 Behold, I am the handmaid of the Lord. May it be done to me according to your word.

Lk. 11:28 Blessed are those who hear the word of God and observe it.

Jn. 1:1 In the beginning was the Word, / and the Word was with God, / and the Word was God.

Jn. 1:14 And the Word became flesh / and made his dwelling among us, / and we saw his glory, / the glory as of the Father's only Son, / full of grace and truth.

Jn. 5:24 Amen, amen, I say to you, whoever hears my word and believes in the one who sent me has eternal life and will not come to condemnation, but has passed from death to life.

Jn. 6:63 It is the spirit that gives life, while the flesh is of no avail. The words I have spoken to you are spirit and life.

Jn. 6:68 Master, to whom shall we go? You have the words of eternal life.

Jn. 8:31-32 If you remain in my word, you will truly be my disciples, and you will know the truth, and the truth will set you free.

Jn. 14:23   Whoever loves me will keep my word, and my Father will love him, and we will come to him and make our dwelling with him.

Jn. 15:3-4   You are already pruned because of the word that I spoke to you. Remain in me, as I remain in you.

Jn. 15:7   If you remain in me and my words remain in you, ask for whatever you want and it will be done for you.

Jn. 17:14   I gave them your word, and the world hated them, because they do not belong to the world any more than I belong to the world.

Jn. 17:17   Consecrate them in the truth. Your word is truth.

Jn. 17:20-21   I pray not only for them, but also for those who will believe in me through their word, so that they may all be one, as you, Father, are in me and I in you, that they also may be in us.

Acts 4:31   As they prayed, the place where they were gathered shook, and they were all filled with the holy Spirit and continued to speak the word of God with boldness.

Rom. 10:8   The word is near you, / in your mouth and in your heart.

Eph. 6:16-17   In all circumstances, hold faith as a shield, to quench all [the] flaming arrows of the evil one. And take the helmet of salvation and the sword of the Spirit, which is the word of God.

Col. 3:16   Let the word of Christ dwell in you richly, as in all wisdom.

Col. 3:17   And whatever you do, in words or in deed, do every-thing in the name of the Lord Jesus, giving thanks to the Father through him.

1Thess. 1:5   For our gospel did not come to you in word alone, but also in power and in the holy Spirit and [with] much conviction.

2Tim. 4:2   Proclaim the word; be persistent whether it is convenient or inconvenient; convince, reprimand, encourage through all patience and teaching.

Heb. 4:12   Indeed, the word of God is living and effective, sharper than any two-edged sword, penetrating even between soul and spirit, joints and marrow, and able to discern reflections and thoughts of the heart.

Ja. 1:21   Humbly welcome the word that has been planted in you and is able to save your souls.

Ja. 1:22-24   Be doers of the word and not hearers only, deluding yourselves. For if anyone is a hearer of the word and not a doer, he is like a man, who looks at his own face in a mirror. He sees himself, then goes off and promptly forgets what he looked like.

1Pet. 1:24-25 All flesh is like grass, / and all its glory like the flower of the field; / the grass withers, / and the flower wilts; / but the word of the Lord remains forever.

1Jn. 2:5-6   Whoever keeps his word, the love of God is truly perfected in him. This is the way we may know that we are in union with him; whoever claims to abide in him ought to live [just] as he lived.

1Jn. 2:14   You are strong and the word of God remains in you, and you have conquered the evil one.

WORTHY

We do not believe in ourselves
until someone reveals
that deep inside us something is valuable,
worth listening to, worthy of our trust,
sacred to our touch.

E.E. Cummings

WORTHY

As I was working on this book, a very special spiritual guide asked, "Did you include the word, *worthy?*" Truly I had thought hard about it for a long time; but now it was time to include it. After all, it is the one word most of us slip up on, for we do not believe ourselves worthy of much.

What does it mean to be worthy? For many of us we think we have to be near perfect. Since none of us are perfect, we believe that we are unworthy. This is especially true in our spiritual lives, filled with so much backsliding and sinfulness. How can we possibly ever be worthy of salvation? Answer … we are not! The One Who Is Worthy, our gracious God who loves us so much, gifts us with the grace we need, redeems us from our sin and opens for us God's own heart! All we have to do is to take the first step, ask for forgiveness, receive God's grace, and take the next step. Do you know who is leading us on this path? God's precious Spirit! All we need to do is follow. God makes us worthy, not by anything we can do, but what God does out of God's love for us! God makes us worthy by dwelling within us and around us.

My heart rises in joy at remembering this, because I know that I am not worthy. I am a work still in progress. God is not finished with me yet! I love the prayer that I say every time before I go to communion:

Lord, I am not worthy to receive you
but only say the word and I shall be healed!

Then I add:

Lord, though unworthy, I must receive You
because without You I am hopeless.
Perfect your love in me!
Amen!

317

I place my whole faith on the Word of
God, Jesus, to make me worthy!

Reflection Questions:

What does the word worthy mean to you?

What or Who makes you worthy?

WORTHY

Ruth 2:13 May I prove worthy of your kindness, my lord; you have comforted me, your servant, with your consoling words; would indeed that I were a servant of yours!

Ps. 119:37 Avert my eyes from what is worthless; / by your way give me life.

Ps. 145:3 Great is the LORD and worthy of high praise; / God's grandeur is beyond understanding.

Ps. 145:13 The Lord is trustworthy in every word, / and faithful in every work.

Wis. 3:5 Chastised a little, they shall be greatly blessed, / because God tried them / and found them worthy of himself.

Sir. 2:5 For in fire gold is tested, / and worthy men in the crucible of humiliation.

Sir. 6:15 A faithful friend is beyond price, / no sum can balance his worth.

Sir. 26:2 A worthy wife brings joy to her husband, / peaceful and full is his life.

Matt. 3:11 I am baptizing you with water, for repentance, but the one who is coming after me is mightier than I. I am not worthy to carry his sandals.

Matt. 8:8 Lord, I am not worthy to have you enter under my roof; only say the word and my servant will be healed.

Matt. 10:11	Whatever town or village you enter, look for a worthy person in it, and stay there until you leave.
Matt. 10:13	If the house is worthy, let your peace come upon it; if not, let your peace return to you.
Matt. 10:37	Whoever loves father or mother more than me is not worthy of me, and whoever loves son or daughter more than me is not worthy of me.
Matt. 10:38	Whoever does not take up his cross and follow after me is not worthy of me.
Lk. 3:16	I am baptizing you with water, but one mightier than I is coming. I am not worthy to loosen the thongs of his sandals. He will baptize you with the holy Spirit and fire.
Lk. 7:6-7	Lord, do not trouble yourself, for I am not worthy to have you enter under my roof. Therefore, I did not consider myself worthy to come to you; but say the word and let my servant be healed.
Acts 5:41	So they left the presence of the Sanhedrin, rejoicing that they had been found worthy to suffer dishonor for the sake of the name.
Rom. 16:2	… that you may receive her in the Lord in a manner worthy of the holy ones, and help her in whatever she may need from you.
Eph. 4:1-3	I, … urge you to live in a manner worthy of the call you have received, with all humility and gentleness, with patience, bearing with one another through love, striving to preserve the unity of the spirit through the bond of peace.

Phil. 1:27   Only, conduct yourselves in a way worthy of the gospel of Christ, so that, whether I come and see you or am absent, I may hear news of you, that you are standing firm in one spirit, with one mind struggling together for the faith of the gospel.

Phil. 4:8   Whatever is true, whatever is honorable, whatever is just, whatever is pure, whatever is lovely, whatever is gracious, if there is any excellence and if there is anything worthy of praise, think about these things.

Col. 1:10   … to live in a manner worthy of the Lord, so as to be fully pleasing, in every good work bearing fruit and growing in the knowledge of God.

1Th. 2:11-12   As you know, we treated each one of you as a father treats his children, exhorting and encouraging you and insisting that you conduct yourselves as worthy of the God who calls you into his kingdom and glory.

2Th. 1:5   This is evidence of the just judgment of God, so that you may be considered worthy of the kingdom of God for which you are suffering.

2Th. 1:11   To this end, we always pray for you, that our God may make you worthy of his calling and powerfully bring to fulfillment every good purpose and every effort of faith.

3Jn. 5-6   Beloved, you are faithful in all you do for the brothers, especially for strangers; they have testified to your love before the church. Please help them in a way worthy of God to continue their journey.

Rev. 3:4   However, you have a few people in Sardis who have not soiled their garments: they will walk with me dressed in white, because they are worthy.

Rev. 4:11   Worthy are you, Lord our God, / to receive glory and honor and power, / for you created all things; / because of your will they came to be and were created.

Rev.5:12   Worthy is the Lamb that was slain / to receive power and riches, wisdom and strength, / honor and glory and blessing.

As we have heard in the past:

Here's the ...

REST OF THE STORY!

The Rest of the Story

NEW AMERICAN BIBLE
EXPLANATIONS

In choosing the bible that I wanted to use for this book I chose the New American Bible. This is the bible I use at Bible study and what we use in our church. In the editing process of the scripture portion I discovered many things I did not know. So I pass this on...
The rest of the story.

* In many cases in the Old Testament the name "LORD" is printed in small capitals to signify use of the divine name in the original Hebrew. Although confusing as to why some and not others I simply followed the direction I had been given. It did call me to an awareness of what I may be missing in the richness of the original Hebrew.

* Also the poetic text must be reprinted in verse format. We used the necessary line breaks with slashes for the purpose of this book.

* The editors of the Greek text placed square brackets [ ] around words or portions of words of which the authenticity is questionable because the evidence of textual witnesses is inconclusive. The same has been done in the translation insofar as it is possible to reproduce this convention in English. It should be possible to read the text either with or without the disputed words, but in English it is not always feasible to provide this alternative, and in some passages the bracketed words must be included to make sense.

The Rest of the Story

WHY 40?

In the gospel of John 21:25 he says:

> There are also many other things that Jesus did,
> but if these were to be described individually,
> I do not think the whole world would contain
> the books that would be written.

Through the years I had gathered to myself scripture passages that I found very useful. At the moment I have worked with 128 words. For retreat groups this has been a great resource for me. Those who work with me have wanted copies of my work. So in the discerning process of how to publish this amount of work, it was suggested that I publish a smaller portion. I have been asked why 40 words? Many of the retreat groups I use this with, number closer to 26-35 people. I always have a few more words than needed so that the last person still has a choice.

40 is the number in the Old Testament that signified a new generation. It seems to be a transitional number that after 40 days, or 40 years ... change happens. A change of heart, a new way of seeing or choosing a different path. People hit the big 40 and ask the questions of themselves: Am I happy with myself? Am I happy with my work? What meaning is in my life? Spiritually, many truly wake up to a new way of seeing.

I used selected passages because these I found to be the most uplifting. There are so many passages, that they all would take up too much room, for the purpose of this book. Books could be written on each and every word. So if you find a different passage that I left out and you like it ... make a note of it for yourself. What I didn't cover in the opening reflection of each word, you can journal for yourself. You will see each word from your own unique perspective. I simply have shared mine. Hopefully, my sharing can be a jumping off point for you. Just a thought, you might find your own pictures that symbolize each word. Create your own version of this book that will encourage you. May you journey deep and discover a richness in yourself, and may you truly become a reflection of

THE WORD,

JESUS!

The Rest of the Story

BACKGROUND ABOUT THE PICTURES

Cover picture: We searched high and low for months for the perfect picture for this book; but could not find it. My precious friend, Brenda-Lea Elbel, set herself on a mission to go find the "tree picture" for this book. On a special Fall adventure, Brenda-Lea accompanied her Mom on a bus trip to enjoy the colorful fall foliage! Brenda-Lea had a whole busload of people looking for the "right tree." After 800 pictures, I chose this one. Looking at the scripture passage on the front of the book, the picture just seemed to be perfect. Here we have *companions on a journey, breaking bread together*, and *sharing their stories*. While all around them and under their feet are hidden acorns from the trees around. Most certainly I can feel the *"presence of God"* in this picture. Thank you Ester Lea Gabrysh, Mary Lee Comer, David and the other most precious companions and to Ester's daughter, Brenda-Lea Elbel, who took the picture and kept the vision!

Anointed: Sheila & Justin Roan brought their little Brennan, to be baptized by Deacon Wesley Rist, a family friend. What a special baptism! A family member even brought holy water from ROME to be used at the baptism!

Believe: My daughters, in their younger years, Laurie & Julie in their favorite tree house. Every tree house can be a

328

special place where one can believe they are capable of being anyone they want to be!

Beloved: Patti & Laurie, a mother-daughter moment. If only our children truly knew how very much they are the beloved of our hearts … just as they are! Just as God loves us … just as we are!

Blessed: Deborah and Wayne Korbar, better known to 'little Brennan' as … 'Nana and Papa.' Brennan is their precious new blessing! Talk about enfleshing the word …"blessing," this little one is perfection. As new grandparents, 'Nana & Papa' are feeling so "blessed" with Brennan!

Called: Sister Dorothy Batto at the Chapel of the Incarnate Word. She was most certainly called by God; and she said, "YES"… over and over again! Sister Dorothy is the creator of the "Sacred Garden," a place one can go for day retreats and spiritual direction. She feels called specifically for women's spirituality.

Chosen: Here is a group of spiritual directors: Patri Williams, Jochelle Demmer, Deborah Korbar, Dean Byers, Ana Frietze, Theresa Luderus, Gloria Rodriguez, Patti King and faithful mentors/teachers, Sister Mary Dumonceaux, Bob Walden and Deborah Hanus. Deborah Hanus leads The Center for the Spiritual and Contemplative Life in San Antonio, Texas. A spiritual place to find deeper prayer, retreat opportunities, and great training for future spiritual directors. These truly are "companions for the journey!"

Courage: Cat Tillotson, a very special waitress, who took little Cayden, my youngest grandchild, under her wings and encouraged him to explore and to not be afraid! You should have seen this child when he discovered bugs! Cayden is not just one of her customers, but those two are like two kids, one a "little older," always on some adventure!

Delight: Kyle Collins at the jetties in Port Aransas, Texas, and loving every minute of it! Ever since Kyle was born, he truly takes delight in everything! He loves to fish, boogie board, and swim in the surf. This place just happens to be a place of "delight" for God ... and me as well!

Dwell: Uncle Mike Hubbell, two years older than his nieces, Laurie & Julie went up on a hill and built their special place as we were building our home! We laughed as they took a broken branch and "planted" it for a tree by their new dwelling. Eventually, the dwelling came down, but the tree grew!

Faith: Kyle Collins, our first grandchild, was fearless! He has tremendous faith in his Grandpa King! Hopefully, surrounded by love, he has learned to fly!

Forgiveness: During a women's retreat at Slumber Falls Camp, a group of daring women walked down a beautiful path that goes down to a river. There was room for one at a time, no baggage! Claudia Garcia is leading the way! Photograph courtesy of Joyce Madden.

Gift: Greg Hubbell, a loving father who, beaming with pride, holds his first daughter, Megan, a precious gift. Greg and his wife Kathy give their daughters, Megan and Ashley, the "gift of their presence" daily. Those girls are growing like beautiful flowers!

Glory: Here our grandchild, Jacob Immel, is totally enjoying himself in the Guadalupe River. Reminds me of those who after being baptized truly emerge glowing in God's glory!

330

Goodness: Cayden & his Daddy, Scott Schultze. These two reflect the desires of our spirits to be close to the goodness of God. Cayden cannot wait until he sees his Daddy's truck coming down the road. He runs to throw himself in his arms!

Grace: Here is one of 800 pictures that Brenda-Lea Elbel took on her fall journey through some "colorful" northeastern states. The statue looks bigger than it really is. Brenda-Lea literally had to lay on the ground to get the picture she desired. What grace she has brought to this book!

Healing: Elizabeth Wilks, great grandmother, had a stroke on her right side. Laurie, Julie and I would go over every week to clean, visit, and cook for her. Grandma complained that no one understood her misery. So on one visit, we donned slings for our right arms and chose to spend the day as Grandma always did … struggling with only our left arms. She laughed so much at us as we tried to put a pillowcase on a pillow, cooking, and eating dinner. She literally had to teach us. What a memorable day for us, and a healing day for Grandma!

Heart: For years Angela Puchot and I worked in youth ministry. Here Angela is doing a skit with Carlos Mendez, on retreat. Carlos had the desire in his heart, to "walk with the cross" through our little town on Good Friday. His dream became a reality, that year and every year after. All the churches in our town come together for our "Cross Walk" every Good Friday. One of my favorite images was of the Baptist minister and our Catholic priest, sharing the load together! From one young man's heart …!

Holy: Twin sisters, Stephanie & Savannah, find themselves pregnant at the same time. Having grown up in each other's shadow, they insisted that their children would not go through that kind of "togetherness." God's sense of humor has Stephanie delivering Gabriel Bumgarner on one day and Savannah delivering Sabin Tamayo 20 hours later. Sabin leans over the top of her cousin to whisper in his ear. Gabriel just lays there thankful to be on holy ground. Brenda-Lea and Michael Elbel, the proud grandparents, could not be happier!

Hope: Kyle and Lani, sharing a quiet moment in the sunshine, with smiles that speak of hope! It doesn't matter what obstacle crops up, these two always say, "It's okay, Grandma … it will be okay!"

Humility: Kyle Collins in all his humility … this is who I am and I love it! All exposed, nothing hidden, … to be happy with who I am, where I am and with what I have!

Joy: "Nana" Deborah Korbar waited a long time for her first grandchild, Brennan. Which one of these two reflects joy the most? Baby Brennan is absolutely as cute as can be; but "Nana" just glows with JOY all the time!

Light: Laurie and Lani Adair, mother and daughter seem to glow with light and peace. Lani could be a flourescent light, for when she lights up with enthusiasm the whole room glows! She gets that from her mother!

Listen: Visiting at another church, a young Jacob Immel, discovered this huge bell. He tried to ring it, but it was just to big. So Deborah Korbar goes over and lifts him up so that he can ring the bell. When they finally succeed, the loudness of the bell has Jacob covering his ears and fleeing for his life. From that moment he called Deborah, "The Bell Ringer!" And she responded, "Bell Ringer's Assistant." Well, Jacob grew up and is now a bell ringer in his own right. You see here Jacob giving Deborah pointers on how to "ring the bells." And if you listen closely you will hear them both giggling as if they know something the rest of us don't!

Love: Grandma, Irene Hubbell with her granddaughter, Julie, the day Julie graduated from A&M! Although that day was special, any time we hold each other in love is a great moment! Both of these women embody the word LOVE in how they care about others!

Mercy: Two grandchildren, Jacob, holding his younger brother Cayden! The love between these two is priceless. Everyone should have an older brother like Jacob. Jacob shows us that "mercy" is both gentle … and strong!

Open: A precious group of friends on a cruise discovering not only the beauty of God's creation, but also the inner beauty of each of our companions! Janice & Mike McMahon, Mike & Patti King, Kathy Gaulke, (her husband Grady was taking the picture) Valerie Maron, John & Mary Chapman, Laura & Wesley Rist and Angela Puchot. To open ourselves to this new opportunity brought great memories! However, we all remember that Mike K. left boot marks as we were going up the ramp to the ship. Mike was not very open at the beginning of this new adventure; but he quickly caught on to the fun! Then we had to drag him off the ship!

Patience: Lani, as so many children do, simply stopped to explore her world! Lani, our only granddaughter, is rarely this still. Yet, I have been so amazed at how she tries to be patient with herself! Most of us do not learn to be this aware of ourselves until much later in life.

Peace:
In our hurried life, Mike, my husband and I took some time to go to the Botanical Gardens in San Antonio. We like to go during the week when it is quieter. I turned around and found Mike sitting quietly just enjoying the peace. We keep dreaming of the day when "all can live in peace!"

Prayer:
If I had to choose someone who is the essence of "prayer" … it would be Angela! There was a story told by a parent of one of Angie's kids, from children's church. When her Dad was trying to explain to the child that her grandfather was with Jesus in heaven, the little girl responded, "Oh, no, Grandpa can't be with Jesus. Jesus lives with Ms. Angie!" Kids know these things. The person behind Angela is Deborah Korbar, a woman who is the "prayer" behind many people! In fact, at our parish, she is the one who sends out the prayer requests to those who will pray for others.

Precious:
Cayden just learning to walk … simply danced into everyone's hearts! One of his first words, which delighted his Mom was …"Precious, Momma!" Cayden would go from table to table at the restaurant waving at everyone repeating this word … precious!

Seek:
Jacob & Cayden at the Christmas crib. Cayden would have crawled in to play with Jesus if we would have let him. Actually, Cayden tried to leave the pew during Church to go visit. Oh, if only we felt that freedom to "seek" God out whenever our hearts wanted to move; but we trained adults bind ourselves way too often!

Servant:	Our Tapestry Retreat Team is a special group of women who do retreats throughout the year. These precious women are true giving servants who share their creativity, joy and love. They encouraged me every step of the way in the creation of this work. It was in one of our planning sessions that this book received it's name! Thank you... Barbara Dybas, Brenda-lea Elbel, Claudia Garcia, Deborah Korbar, Irene Martinez, Angela Puchot, and Louise Scott. I am so blessed to be a part of you.
Soul:	Lani contemplating ... what? Whatever it was, it was deep for such a little one! Oh, to be that quiet and centered to listen to our soul. To be that wrapped in the present moment!
Spirit:	Gloria Bocanegra, Pat Glaze, Phyllis Groff, Patti King, Darlene Koehler, Mary Mainz, Alice, Barbara , Ginger McDowell, Chickie McManus, Angie Puchot, Pat Shedrock, Jo Stuart, Darnell Vader, and Helen Zenner. A precious group of women who came together to perform at an evening, honoring our parish pastor, Father Peter McKenna. All lay women, all active with jobs and families simply coming forth in a spirit of fellowship and fun. There is no doubt that the "spirit" is alive in our parish!
Strength:	Jacob was helping his cousin Lani on the ice skating rink. When she needed strength he was there! Just like God is there for us! My heart is always uplifted when I observe the kids being strength for each other.
Trust:	Lani simply crawled into her diaper box and went to sleep. However, she didn't tell anyone; and her Mom was going crazy looking for her! Oh, to be so trusting that I could just curl up anywhere and sleep peacefully.

Truth:	Rev. Alois Goertz, Rev. Carlos Velasquez, Mike King, Michael Wagner and teens at Mass at Vesper Point, Slumber Falls Camp. Our lives truly speak the truth we believe. These are four very special men who embody "truth."
Wisdom:	My husband, Michael and our daughter, Julie in Arkansas. These two people are great sources of wisdom for me. Although, that day I was taking the picture and questioning their wisdom of getting too close to the edge!
Word:	Rev. Peter McKenna and his brother Rev. Enda McKenna are two very special people who enflesh the "WORD" in their lives! Father Enda baptized our daughter Laurie. Father Peter baptized our grandson Jacob. Under the encouragement of both, I have grown in the WORD of God!
Worthy:	Sister Dorothy Batto, the director of the "Sacred Garden," on the campus of Incarnate Word, 4503 Broadway, San Antonio. Tx 78209. The word worthy was her suggestion for this book. She has found that feeling worthy is a deep problem for so many people, especially women. She is good at helping people discover their true worth!

Works Cited

Calvi, John, The Spirit Winds Poetry of Gods Messages: A Daily Poetry Book, Paula A Timpson, p.158,1Universe, 2002.

Confucius, Fire of Grace: The Healing Power of Forgiveness, Richard W. Rouse, p.1, Augsburg Books, 2005.

De Chardin, Pierre Teilhard, The Green Bible, Stephen B. Sharper & Hillary Cunningham, p.71, Lantern Books, 2002.

DeSales, St. Francis, Zen Master Next Door, Edward G. Kardas, p.197 Humanics Publishing Group, 2009.

E.E. Cummings, The Wisdom of Listening, Mark Brady, p.5, Wisdom Publications, 2006.

Elizabeth of the Trinity, Blessed. At Prayer with the Saints, Compiled by Anthony F. Chiffolo, p.119, Liguori Press,1998.

Emerson, Ralph Waldo, http://thinkexist.com

Evdokimov, Paul, www.ocytoronto.org/resources/prayer.htm

Hanh, Thich Nhat, We Walk the Path Together: Learning from Thich Nhat Hanh and Meister Eckhart, Brian J. Pierce, p.38, Orbis Books, 2005.

Hanus, Deborah, The Center for Spiritual Growth and the Contemplative Life Newsletter, Fall 2009.

Hurnard, Hannah, Hind's Feet on High Places, Tyndale House Publisher,1997.

Irenaeus,St., What Makes Us Catholic, Thomas Grooma, p.60, Harper Collins, 2003.

Jerome, St., At Prayer with the Saints, complied by Anthony F. Chiffolo, p.71 Liguori Press, 1998.

John of the Cross, <u>Praying with John of the Cross</u>, Wayne Simsic, p.89 St. Mary's Press,1993.

Julian of Norwich, <u>Praying with Julian of Norwich</u>, Gloria Durka, p.46, St. Mary's Press,1989. <u>Meditations with Julian of Norwich</u>, Brendon Doyle, p.60, Inner Traditions/Bear& Company,1983.

Keller, Helen, <u>The Open Door</u>, Helen Keller, p.139, Doubleday, 1957.

Kingsley, Charles, <u>Daily Thoughts</u>, Charles Kingsley, p.41, BiblioBazaar.LLC, 2009.

Kowalkska, St. Maria Faustina, <u>www.trustandmercy.com/divinemercyprayers/</u> <u>St.Faustina</u>

Kubler-Ross, Elisabeth, <u>http://thinkexist.com/quotes/Elisabeth_Kubler-Ross</u>

Lennon, John, <u>John Lennon's Secret</u>, David Stuart Ryan, p.247, Kozmik Press,1982.

Mandela, Nelson, <u>Be Your Best! A Roadmap to Living a Healthy, Balanced & Fulfilling Life,</u> Jeff Thibodeau, p.87, Dog Ear Publishing, 2007.

Neri, St. Phillip, <u>The New Encyclopedia of Christian Quotations</u>, Mark Water, p.722 Baker Books 2001.

Nouwen, Henri, <u>The Westminster Collection of Christian Quotations</u>, Martin Manser, p.29, Westminster John Knox Press, 2001

Rose of Lima, St., <u>The Book of Positive Quotations</u>, John Cook, Steve Deger, Leslie Ann Gibson, p.676, Fairview Press, 2007.

Rupp, Joyce, <u>The Star in My Heart</u>, p.87, Sorin Books, 2004.

Ruskin, John, <u>A Trail of Light</u>, Don Bosco Salesian Bulletin

Teresa of Avila, <u>The Collected Works of St. Teresa of Avila</u>, Kieran Kavanaugh, p.96 Institute of Carmelite Studies,1980. <u>The Interior Castle</u>, translated by Mirabai Starr, p.260 Penguin Group, 2004.

Praying with Teresa of Avila, Rosemary Broughton, p.61, 85 and 106, Saint Mary's Press,1990.

Teresa of Calcutta, Mother, Love, a Fruit always in Season: Daily Meditations from the words of Mother Teresa, Dorothy Hunt, p.116, Ignatius Press, 1987.
No Greater Love, Becky Benenate, Joseph Durepas, p.16, 33, 53, New World Library, 2002.

Therese of Lisieux, Praying with Therese of Lisieux, Joseph Schmidt, p.106, St. Mary's Press,1992.

Wiederkehr, Macrina, Seven Sacred Pauses, Macrina Wiederkehr, p.59, Sorin Books, 2008.

Williamson, Marianne, A Return to Love: Reflections on the Principles of Course of Miracles, p.165, New York:Harper Collins,1992.

MUSIC

Kauffman, David, "Be Still," CD Be Still
"I Think of You with Love" from the CD Surrender
"Purify My Heart," from the CD Surrender

"I Will Make This Day My Prayer," from the CD Be Still Words and Music by David Kauffman ©2005 GFTSM Publishing Co (BMI) Administered by Music Services, Nashville, Tn. All Rights Reserved. Used with permission. www.goodforthesoul.com 1.88.759.5805

Poirier, Michael John "Ocean of Mercy," by Michael John Poirier © 1992, Michael John Poirier, published by Prayer Songs Publishing Company. Licensing agent: Franklin Park Illinois. www.wlpmusic.com All rights reserved. Used by permission.

For Michael John Poirier's songs, you can find them available through:
World Library Publications, 800-566-6150 or online at www.wlpmusic.com

Viva Bookstore, 8407 Broadway, San Antonio, Texas 78209

EXPERIENCES WITH THE WORD

******

I received the word "Dwelling" during the Word Ceremony. I was struggling with a medical decision during this time. When I received this word, the scripture verses that followed addressed my fears and helped me make a decision. I was in awe at how that one word- Dwelling- affected my life. It stays with me to this day reminding me that my body is a temple and that God is Dwelling within me.

Brenda-Lea Elbel
Schoertz, Tx.

****

I remember receiving the word "Delight" once at a retreat. At the time it was a great encouragement to me to think that God may actually delight in me and want me to be happy and rejoice in this life. Especially since at the time I was filled with so much sadness and self-recrimination. I always have the feeling of being personally touched by God in the word I receive.

Joyce Madden
Sutherland Springs, Tx.

****

I have been given many words throughout my life. But the word that touched the core of my being. Peace given to me at an Acts Retreat. I felt that it was a message and gift from God. In time, I realized that this is what has guided me through fears and storms. Words are given to us to be cherished, nourished and shared with each other and the world. This mission was given to my sister Patti. I would encourage each person to step out in faith and receive what word God would give to you!

Angie Puchot
La Vernia, Tx.

ABOUT THE AUTHOR

Patti King has spent 35 years in religious education and youth ministry. Currently, she is involved as a spiritual director, retreat work, and her love ... bible study! Although deeply involved in her faith community, she believes that her spirituality is truly "lived out" in everyday, family life. Happily married for 39 years, a mother of two and grandmother of four, Patti has special stories of God breaking through in those ordinary but precious times ... lots of acorns of wisdom!

Printed in the United States
By Bookmasters